DK EYE

KT-527-443

TOP10
ORLANDO

9030 00006 9635 6

LONDON BOROUGH OF WANDSWORTH

9030 00006 9635 6	
Askews & Holts	14-Nov-2019
917.5924	£8.99
	WW19010564

Top 10 Orlando Highlights

The Top 10 of Everything

CONTENTS

Orlando Area by Area

Streetsmart

Within each Top 10 list in this book, no hierarchy of quality or popularity is implied. All 10 are, in the editor's opinion, of roughly equal merit.
Throughout this book, floors are referred to in accordance with American usage; i.e., the "first floor" is at ground level.

Title page, front cover and spine Palm-fringed Lake Eola at dusk
Back cover, clockwise from top left Downtown cityscape; Cocoa Beach pier; lush golf course; Lake Eola; ICON Orlando™

The information in this DK Eyewitness Top 10 Travel Guide is checked regularly. Every effort has been made to ensure that this book is as up-to-date as possible at the time of going to press. Some details, however, such as telephone numbers, opening hours, prices, gallery hanging arrangements and travel information, are liable to change. The publishers cannot accept responsibility for any consequences arising from the use of this book, nor for any material on third party websites, and cannot guarantee that any website address in this book will be a suitable source of travel information. We value the views and suggestions of our readers very highly. Please write to: Publisher, DK Eyewitness Travel Guides, Dorling Kindersley, 80 Strand, London WC2R 0RL, Great Britain, or email travelguides@dk.com

Welcome to
Orlando

While it may have started with a mouse, the Orlando experience has become increasingly diverse. It's expanded far beyond its thrilling theme parks, with attractions that include a sophisticated dining scene, luxurious lodgings, lively bars and nightclubs, and some of the most stunning parks and preserves in Florida. With Eyewitness Top 10 Orlando, it's yours to explore.

Central Florida lays claim to six of the world's top thrill-filled theme parks (**Magic Kingdom® Park** is the most visited), along with a dizzying array of smaller distractions. Only here is it possible to save the world alongside Optimus Prime at **Universal Studios Florida™**, narrowly escape from Gringotts Bank with a fire-breathing dragon on your heels at **The Wizarding World of Harry Potter™**, head out on a nighttime safari at **Disney's Animal Kingdom®**, and immerse yourself in the cultures of 11 nations at **Epcot®** – all within the space of a week.

In contrast to this mass appeal, an emerging sophistication is now apparent, with a swath of luxury hotels and resorts moving in. Their lounges, spas, and award-winning restaurants are increasingly popular with more affluent park-goers. Away from the theme parks, the area also boasts some superb natural attractions, including **Merritt Island National Wildlife Refuge** – the second-largest reserve in Florida.

Whether you're visiting for a weekend or a week, our Top 10 guide brings together the best of everything the city has to offer, from thrill rides and water parks to five-star dining and manatee-spotting tours. The guide has useful tips throughout, from seeking out what's free to avoiding the crowds, plus five easy-to-follow itineraries, designed to tie together a clutch of sights in a short space of time. Add inspiring photography and detailed maps, and you've got the essential travel companion. **Enjoy the book, and enjoy Orlando**.

Clockwise from top: **Themed topiary at the Magic Kingdom® Park, carvings on the Tree of Life at Disney's Animal Kingdom® Park, Spaceship Earth at Epcot®, view of Downtown Orlando, entrance to Seuss Landing at Universal's Islands of Adventure™, the Flight of Passage ride at Pandora – The World of Avatar, Hollywood Rip Ride Rockit® at Universal Studios Florida™**

Exploring Orlando

Visitors to Orlando will never find themselves stuck for things to see and do. Whether you're here for a short stay or long vacation, making the most of your time is key. Here are some ideas for two- and four-day tours of Orlando.

Climb aboard a runaway mine train on the thrilling Big Thunder Mountain Railroad at the Magic Kingdom®.

Two Days in Orlando

Day ❶
MORNING

Begin at the **Magic Kingdom® Park** *(see pp12–15)*, strolling down Main Street U.S.A.®, and stopping for a photo in front of Cinderella Castle. Then blast your way through Buzz Lightyear's Space Ranger Spin, and rocket through the cosmos on Space Mountain®. Stop for lunch at Columbia Harbour House (Liberty Square, Magic Kingdom® Park).

AFTERNOON

Continue counterclockwise around the park, taking a quick world tour aboard It's a Small World, before braving the Haunted Mansion® and riding a runaway mine train at Big Thunder Mountain Railroad. Prepare to get soaked at Splash Mountain®, and then go on to plunder and pillage on Pirates of the Caribbean®. Join the Disney Princesses for a grand dinner surrounded by stone archways and stained-glass windows at Cinderella's Royal Table *(see p101)*. Younger guests should dress up for the occasion. Afterward, head back to your hotel for a well-deserved rest.

Day ❷
MORNING

Begin at **Universal's Islands of Adventure™** *(see pp30–33)*, where the Incredible Hulk Coaster® and The Amazing Adventures of Spider-Man® are first on the list. Explore Skull Island: Reign of Kong™, then Jurassic Park River Adventure®, before entering **The Wizarding World of Harry Potter™** *(see pp34–5)*. Ride Harry Potter and the Forbidden Journey™, explore the village of Hogsmeade™, then hop aboard the Hogwarts™ Express for more Potter at **Universal Studios Florida™** *(see pp26–9)*.

AFTERNOON

Lunch at the Leaky Cauldron, and then spend some time exploring the shops on Diagon Alley™. Ride Harry Potter and the Escape from Gringotts™ before returning to Universal Studios Florida™. Finish the day with dinner at one of the many restaurants in **CityWalk™**.

Fireworks light up the sky at *Happily Ever After* in the Magic Kingdom®.

making sure to catch *Beauty and the Beast Live on Stage* and the *Indiana Jones™ Epic Stunt Spectacular*.

AFTERNOON
Have an early lunch at the Hollywood Brown Derby *(see p101)*, before trying to catch any shows you didn't fit in earlier. Afterward, enjoy Star Tours® and Toy Story Land. Exit the park, taking a water taxi to **Disney's BoardWalk** *(see p96)*. Rent a surrey bike for a ride around, then stop for dinner before taking a seat on the lawn at 9pm to watch the famous IllumiNations: Reflections of Earth at Epcot® *(see p99)*.

Four Days in Orlando

Day ❶
MORNING
Follow the morning section of Day 1 for the two-day itinerary.

AFTERNOON
After lunch, take your time with the smaller attractions, such as Mad Tea Party, Tomorrowland® Transit Authority PeopleMover, Peter Pan's Flight, the Walt Disney World® Railroad, and Hall of Presidents. Catch the 3pm parade, and any rides left on your must-see list, before exiting the park. Take the monorail to **Disney's Grand Floridian Resort & Spa** for dinner at Narcoossee's *(see p100)*, and end the day watching the sky light up with fireworks over the Magic Kingdom® from the restaurant's deck.

Day ❷
MORNING
Start the day at Disney's Hollywood Studios® *(see pp20–21)*, riding Twilight Zone Tower of Terror™ and Rock 'n' Roller Coaster® before the lines get too long. Check the show schedule,

Day ❸
Follow Day 2 of the two-day itinerary.

Day ❹
MORNING
Get an early start at **Disney's Animal Kingdom®** *(see pp22–3)*, heading directly to Kilimanjaro Safaris® when the animals are most visible. Walk the Pangani Forest Exploration Trail®, taking in all the details and enjoy the thrill ride, Avatar Flight of Passage at Pandora - The World of Avatar.

AFTERNOON
Ride Kali River Rapids® and enjoy Expedition Everest after lunch, then catch a showing of the *Festival of the Lion King* or *Finding Nemo – The Musical*. Afterward, take a ride on DINOSAUR, and then start making your way to **Disney Springs™** *(see p95)*. Grab dinner in one of the restaurants, and then indulge in some shopping at Town Center and Marketplace before heading back to your hotel.

Top 10 Orlando Highlights

Exterior of Spaceship Earth at Epcot®

Orlando Highlights

Orlando's stunning transformation over the last 40 years – from plain Jane to worldly beauty – shows no signs of stopping. Millions of tourists are seduced every year by its ever-evolving range of thrilling theme parks, its sophisticated resorts, superb dining scene, and happening nightclubs. Here are the Top 10 sights and attractions – Orlando's best of the best.

1 Magic Kingdom® Park

The park that started Disney's Florida empire blends fantasy, adventure, and a throwback vision of the future into a magical collection of rides and attractions (see pp12–15).

Epcot® 2

This Disney park features tech-inspired thrill rides and attractions in Future World, plus the culture, architecture, and cuisine of 11 nations in World Showcase (see pp16–19).

3 Disney's Hollywood Studios®

Visit the unofficial Star Wars Land and meet Kylo Ren and Chewbacca. Also catch the *Star Wars: A Galaxy Far, Far Away* stage show (see pp20–21).

Disney's Animal Kingdom® Park 4

Visitors are brought face to face with the wild world of animals, which lurk (often hidden) amid exotic, meticulously re-created landscapes (see pp22–3).

5 Universal Studios Florida™

The streetscapes and special effects bring the silver screen to life in this movie and TV studio theme park. Ride with the Simpsons, save the world with the Transformers, or party with the Minions (see pp26–9).

6 Universal's Islands of Adventure™

Re-creations of magical, far-off lands – from Jurassic Park to Seussian scenes – pack this adrenaline-thrill-filled theme park. Adults and children alike will delight in seeing their favorite movies come to life (see pp30–33).

7 The Wizarding World of Harry Potter™

Step into Diagon Alley or Hogsmeade to join in the famous wizard's adventures at these two parks, linked by the Hogwarts™ Express (see pp34–5).

8 LEGOLAND®

Aimed at younger kids, this theme park and adjacent water park are crammed with rides, shows, and colorful brick creations (see pp36–7).

9 Merritt Island

Close to the Kennedy Space Center Visitor Complex, this wild-life refuge, with an array of birds, fish, mammals, and reptiles, offers a great opportunity to explore Florida's coastline (see pp38–9).

10 Kennedy Space Center Visitor Complex

The Space Center is a stellar attraction, complete with exhibits on the cosmos, live rocket launches, encounters with astronauts, and tours (see pp40–43).

TOP 10 ⭐ Magic Kingdom® Park

Walt Disney's first Florida theme park opened in 1971 as a spin-off of California's Disneyland® Park, and was envisaged as a place where dreams could come true, even if only for a little while. Nowadays, the Magic Kingdom® is the most popular of all Disney parks, welcoming some 20 million guests every year (over 50,000 each day). With more than 40 major attractions and countless smaller ones, this is a true fantasy land for visitors of any age.

① Pirates of the Caribbean®

Timbers are a-shiver as your boat cruises past a town under siege from a band of rum-soaked, Audio-Animatronic® buccaneers **(below)**. Dank dungeons, yo-ho-hos, and brazen wenches – all scurvy pirate life is here.

② Buzz Lightyear's Space Ranger Spin

Use the laser cannons on the dashboard to set off sight-and-sound effects as you hurtle through the sky and help *Toy Story*'s famous hero save the world.

③ Peter Pan's Flight

A flying pirate galleon soars over the nighttime sights of London and arrives in Never Land, where Peter Pan battles Captain Hook to save Wendy and her brothers.

④ Splash Mountain®

Disney's 1946 movie *Song of the South* inspires this flume ride **(above)** – Brer Rabbit leads you through swamps, caves, and "the Laughing Place." Expect to get soaked at the steep and speedy 52-ft (16-m) climax.

⑤ The Jungle Cruise

Cruise through the African Congo, the Amazon rain-forest, and along the Egyptian Nile, where animatronic animals roam free. The real appeal of this classic ride **(below)** is the captain's corny commentary.

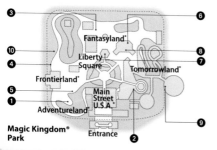

Magic Kingdom®
Park

NEED TO KNOW

MAP F1 ■ World Drive
■ 407-824-4321 ■ www.
disneyworld.com

Open 9am–7pm
daily, with extended
seasonal hours

Adm (1-day ticket, park
specific): adults $116–
137; children (3–9)
$110–132 (incl tax);
under-3s go free

*Splash Mountain®, Big
Thunder Railroad, Space
Mountain®:* min height
40 inches (102 cm)

■ FastPass+ *(see p140)*
cuts the time spent
standing in line. Up to
3 FastPass+ selections
can be made online.

■ Guests of Disney's
official resorts get more
time in the parks: every
day one park opens
early or closes later.

■ MagicBands allow
Disney resort guests to
tap to enter their hotel
room, charge meals,
enter the parks, make
FastPass+ reservations,
and more. Guests staying
elsewhere can buy
them ($14.99–24.99)
for use in the parks.

8 The Many Adventures of Winnie the Pooh

Pooh, Eeyore, and a host
of A. A. Milne's lovable
characters come to life
in this tranquil ride
through the Hundred
Acre Wood.

9 Space Mountain®

Orlando's first in-the-dark
roller coaster is a rocket
ride through hairpin turns
and drops at what feels
like breakneck speed.
Galactic details and
sound effects enhance
this classic thrill ride.

6 Seven Dwarfs Mine Train

This twisty coaster is
good for visitors who are
not up to the park's most
intense rides, as it slows
down to trundle through
the Enchanted Forest
and diamond mines.

7 Prince Charming Regal Carrousel

This restored 1917
carousel is a sight to
behold, with handsome
wooden horses and an
organ that plays Disney
classics. Kids – and
nostalgic adults – love it.

10 Big Thunder Mountain Railroad

Not the fastest coaster,
(above) but the turns and
dips, and realistic scenery,
combine to make this an
exciting trip on a run-
away mine train through
gold-rush country.

Park Guide

It takes more than 20
minutes to get from the
parking lots (via tram,
boat, or monorail) to
the Magic Kingdom®
entrance. Once inside,
pick up a guide map
and times guide. You
can access real-time
info, including wait
times, on your smart-
phone with the My
Disney Experience app.
You'll need at least a
day, preferably two, to
fully experience the
Magic Kingdom®.

Shows and Next Best Rides

Colorful characters from It's a Small World

1 It's a Small World

Small kids and nostalgic adults alike adore this slow cruise around the world, where colorfully costumed characters portray the world's cultures. There's just no avoiding it: the catchy theme tune will stick in your head for months.

2 Happily Ever After

This dazzling show lights up the sky nightly during summer months and school holidays (and on select nights at other times of the year). Liberty Square, the main gates, and Frontierland® are the best areas in the park to take in the display. Outside the park, views are best from Disney's Contemporary Resort, Wilderness Lodge, Grand Floridian Resort & Spa, and Polynesian Village.

3 Cinderella Castle

Standing at 185 ft (56 m) high, this park icon is a sight to behold. Complete with Gothic spires, it's the quintessential fairy-tale castle, reminiscent of

Cinderella Castle

Neuschwanstein, King Ludwig of Bavaria's creation. Inside is Cinderella's Royal Table (see p101), the most sought-after dining experience in Walt Disney World®.

4 Under the Sea – Journey of the Little Mermaid

Embark on a musical underwater adventure with this ride, which takes you below the waves without getting wet. The ride recreates scenes from the Disney classic with the help of animatronics and video. Afterwards, visit Ariel's Grotto and spend some time with your favorite mermaid.

5 Walt Disney World® Railroad

The antique steam-driven trains that travel this 1.5-mile (2-km) perimeter track offer a good overview of the park's sights, but more importantly allow you to get around without the legwork. The 20-minute ride stops at Walt Disney World® Railroad Station, Main Street U.S.A.®, Frontierland®, and magical Fantasyland®.

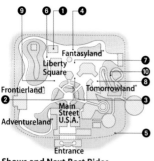

Shows and Next Best Rides

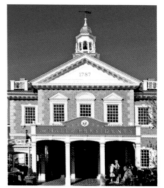

Entrance to the Hall of Presidents

6 Haunted Mansion®

Ghosts come out to socialize on this slow-moving Doom Buggy ride in the dark. More amusing than scary (for all but younger children), it's a cult classic, and one of the most popular rides in the park.

Screening of Mickey's PhilharMagic

7 Mickey's PhilharMagic

Disney magic meets Disney music in a 3-D movie spectacular starring Mickey Mouse, Donald Duck, and other favorite Disney characters animated in a way never seen before. It is located in the PhilharMagic concert hall in Fantasyland®.

8 Mad Tea Party

Round and round you go, spinning in whimsically painted pastel-colored teacups on spinning platforms. Riders control how much their own teacups spin on this usually tame ride, but if you get dizzy easily, this may not be for you.

9 Hall of Presidents

All 45 US presidents are represented by fluid Audio-Animatronics® in this fascinating educational show that highlights the wizardry of Walt Disney Imagineers.

10 Tomorrowland® Transit Authority PeopleMover

High above the ground, this 10-minute narrated tour of Tomorrowland® offers some of the best views in the park (especially after dark), including a peek inside Space Mountain®.

MAGIC KINGDOM® PARADES

Parades are a vital part of the Disney experience. There's one each afternoon, throughout the summer, on holidays, and select evenings during the year. The musical celebrations are held at the Cinderella Castle stage, featuring popular Disney characters. To honor Walt Disney's imagination, the castle is transformed into a light-projection canvas. Tinker Bell splashes pixie dust atop the castle, Alice pops down to Wonderland, and Simba strolls the Savanna bringing the tales to life. Main Street, U.S.A.® gets crowded for parades and musical performances. Arrive early to secure a spot in front of the castle, in Town Square, or Frontierland®. If you can't stay until after dark, be sure to catch Disney's Festival of Fantasy parade (3pm daily), featuring favorite characters, street performers, and spectacular, whimsical floats.

📷10 ⭐ Epcot®

Walt Disney imagined Epcot® (Experimental Prototype Community of Tomorrow) as a town where people could live, work, and play in technological splendor. After his death in 1966, the idea changed dramatically, and Epcot® opened in 1982 as a theme park, pairing Future World (exploring technology and education) with World Showcase (devoted to various nations). Be warned, the park is vast – some joke that its name is an acronym for "Every Person Comes Out Tired."

1 Turtle Talk with Crush

Kids in the audience ask Crush questions during this unique, unscripted, digitally animated 10-minute show. Characters from both *Finding Nemo* and *Finding Dory* are featured.

4 Spaceship Earth

The ride inside isn't the most exciting, but this gigantic geosphere (**right**), symbol of Epcot®, is an engineering marvel. Its 11,324 aluminum panels absorb the rain rather than letting it run off.

2 Mission: SPACE®

This popular thrill ride (**above**) takes you on a high-intensity journey into space with a crash landing on Mars. There are two versions to choose from, depending on how prone to motion sickness you are.

5 Soarin' Around the World

Feel the exhilarating rush of this free-flying hang-gliding adventure over several magnificent landscapes around the globe. You must be 40 inches (102 cm) tall.

3 Journey into Imagination with Figment

An open house at Dr. Channing's Imagination Institute is turned inside out by Figment, a playful purple dragon. Figment causes chaos as the tour visits five sensory-themed labs, before moving to the dragon's own upside-down home.

6 Living with the Land

The best of this vast pavilion's exhibits is a 13-minute boat ride (**left**) through three diverse environments – rainforest, desert, and prairie. It's followed by a look at agricultural experiments, including hydroponics and gardening in simulated Martian soil.

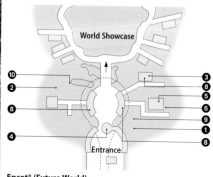

Epcot® (Future World)

8 Innoventions

A good place to seek refuge from the heat, this exhibit offers an ever-changing lineup of interactive experiences, such as Colortopia, which explores color, and StormStruck, where you get to see and feel the effects of hurricane-force winds.

10 Test Track

After designing and digitally road testing your own concept car, you can hop aboard a SIM Car for a driving adventure that takes you flying along straightaways and steep curves, reaching speeds of 65 mph (104 km/h). You must be at least 40 inches (102 cm) tall.

9 The Seas with Nemo & Friends

Board a "clamobile" and join an undersea adventure with some familiar friends to help find Nemo. Also in this pavilion **(right)** are *Turtle Talk with Crush* and Sea Base Alpha.

7 Disney & Pixar Short Film Festival

Experience popular short films like never before – in 4D. Fun for all ages.

NEED TO KNOW

MAP G2 ■ Epcot Center Dr, Walt Disney World® Resort ■ 407-824-4321 ■ www.disneyworld.com

Future World: open 9am–9:30pm daily

World Showcase: open 11am–9:30pm daily, with extended seasonal hours; adm (1-day ticket, park specific): adults $116–137, children (3–9) $110–132 (incl tax), under-3s go free

Test Track, Innoventions, Soarin' Around the World: ages 8 and over

Mission: SPACE®: ages 12 and over

■ Make FastPass+ *(see p140)* reservations ahead.

■ World Showcase restaurants are popular, not just with park-goers – reserve in advance.

■ Take at least 2 days to make the most of this park.

Park Guide
The main entrance is handy for Future World, where nine pavilions encircle Spaceship Earth. World Showcase Lagoon and the 11 nations beyond are farther, though boat shuttles run from Showcase Plaza to the Germany and Morocco pavilions. A second entrance, at International Gateway, is accessible from Disney's Yacht Club, Beach Club, and BoardWalk Inn resorts.

World Showcase Pavilions

Ming temple and ceremonial entrance gate into the China pavilion

 China

The CircleVision movie, *Reflections of China*, is a fascinating journey through China's natural and man-made riches. The pavilion features a 15th-century Ming dynasty temple, a ceremonial gate, and tranquil gardens. The Yong Feng Shangdian Department Store is a treasure trove of Asian goodies. Try not to miss the dynamic Dragon Legend Acrobats, who perform several times each day.

 Germany

In this archetypal German village, where Oktoberfest is celebrated year-round, you'll find a miniature model railroad, including a wonderfully detailed Bavarian Village. The Biergarten restaurant (with live brass band music) serves traditional food, and shops sell everything from Hummel figurines to wines and cuckoo clocks.

 Mexico

Surrounded by jungle landscaping stands an immense Mayan temple, inside of which mariachi bands play under a perpetually starlit sky. The plaza bustles with artisans peddling their wares. Visit the Mexican countryside aboard the Gran Fiesta Tour, an 8-minute boat ride with an animated element starring Donald Duck.

 Canada

The star attraction here is the inspirational 360-degree CircleVision movie, *O Canada!*, which reveals some of the country's scenic wonders. Outside, Canada's rugged terrain is convincingly re-created. You can explore gardens based on Victoria's Butchart Gardens, a replica of an indigenous Canadian village, and the Northwest Mercantile store, selling crafts and maple syrup.

Canada totem pole

 American Adventure

Enhance your knowledge of US history in a 30-minute dramatization featuring Audio-Animatronic® actors. Mark Twain and Benjamin Franklin explain key events such as the writing of the Declaration of Independence, while Susan B. Anthony speaks out for women's rights. The Voices of Liberty singers perform in the main hall of the pavilion, which is modeled on Philadelphia's Liberty Hall.

⑥ Japan

A breathtaking five-story pagoda, based on Nara's 8th-century Horyuji temple, forms the centerpiece of this architecturally stunning pavilion. The traditional Japanese gardens are also impressive, and great for escaping the crowds. The peace is occasionally broken by the beat of drums – the Matsuriza troupe put on one of the best shows in Epcot®.

DINING IN ITALY

Italy, the 11th pavilion at Epcot®, is home to some of the best food outlets in the complex. Enjoy gelato while strolling around re-creations of the Campanile of St. Mark's Square and the Doge's Palace in Venice, or sit down to authentic Italian food in Tutto Italia Ristorante. The pizzas at Via Napoli (see p101) are cooked in wood-fired brick ovens with giant, open-mouthed terra-cotta faces on the front.

⑦ Morocco

Look for the Koutoubia minaret, a replica of the tower from a 12th-century mosque in Marrakesh. Inside this exotic pavilion, the typical souk architecture is embellished by beautiful carvings and mosaics. The authentic marketplace is full of hard-to-resist crafts sold by "merchants," and you can see carpets being woven. Moroccan cuisine is served in Restaurant Marrakesh (see p101).

Tiled water fountain, Morocco

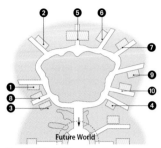

Epcot® (World Showcase)

⑧ Norway

In the cobblestone courtyard of Norway's pavilion, the residents of Arendelle are celebrating the Winter in Summer Festival. Hop aboard a log for a *Frozen*-themed snowy ride. Akershus Royal Banquet Hall (a replica of Oslo's 14th-century castle) houses a restaurant.

Parisian-style dining, France

⑨ France

This beautiful pavilion sports a scale replica of the Eiffel Tower among many other sights focused on French art, architecture, and literature. Another highlight is *Impressions de France*, an 18-minute, five-screen movie that sweeps through glorious landscapes, accompanied by music by French composers.

⑩ United Kingdom

Examples of typical British architecture through the ages line the cobblestone streets here. Apart from shops selling quintessential British merchandise (teas, china, and more), there's also a maze and a bandstand with daily live music.

🔟 ⭐ Disney's Hollywood Studios®

From the set-like streetscapes to its lineup of thrilling rides and fantastic stage productions – all based on blockbuster movies and TV shows – Disney's Hollywood Studios® aims to bring the magic of the movies to life. Since its opening in 1989, the park has continued to evolve, merging the nostalgic references to Hollywood's heyday with an increasing emphasis on the *Star Wars* films, making this a must for anyone with even a remote interest in the movies.

1 Voyage of the Little Mermaid

This charming undersea stage show uses puppets, live performers, amazing special effects, and clips from the animated movie to tell Ariel's story.

2 Star Tours®

Climb in and buckle up: your 40-seat spacecraft is going on a *Star Wars*-inspired, flight-motion simulated 3-D journey, riddled with dips, bumps, and laser fire.

3 Indiana Jones™ Epic Stunt Spectacular

Indy's action-packed day is full of thrills and spills, and near-death encounters **(above)**. A stunt coordinator explains how it's all done.

4 Toy Story Land

Enjoy the estate of *Toy Story* where Woody, Jessie and their friends have fun in Andy's backyard. Rides here **(left)** include Slinky Dog Dash and Alien Swirling Saucers.

5 Beauty and the Beast Live on Stage

The music from the movie is enough to sell this Broadway-style show, but the sets, costumes, and production numbers are spectacular, too.

NEED TO KNOW

MAP G2 ▪ Epcot Resorts Blvd ▪ 407-824-4321 ▪ www.disneyworld.com

Open 9am–7pm; sometimes later

Adm (1-day ticket, park-specific): adults $116–137; children (3–9) $110–132 (incl tax); under-3s go free

Rock 'n' Roller Coaster® Starring Aerosmith: min height 48 inches (122 cm)

Twilight Zone Tower of Terror™ and *Star Tours®:* min height 40 inches (102 cm)

▪ Eat sitting in a 1950s-style convertible while watching B-movies at the Sci-Fi Dine-In Theater.

▪ Specialty tours include a 7-hour Backstage Magic Tour at Disney's Hollywood Studios®, Epcot®, and the Magic Kingdom® *(see p141).*

Park Guide

Pick up a map from guest services, by the entrance. For real-time information on schedules, wait times, visiting celebrities, and closures, download the My Disney Experience app. This park tends to be less busy at the start of the week, when many visitors hit the Magic Kingdom® and Epcot®, and it can easily be tackled in one day.

⑨ Muppet™ Vision 3-D

Miss Piggy, Kermit, and the rest of the crew star in a show celebrating both Jim Henson's legacy and Disney's own special-effects wizardry and Audio-Animatronics® **(below)**.

⑩ Jedi Training: Trials of the Temple

Young padawans must sign up early for this 20-minute training session in the art of fighting with a light saber, led by a Jedi Master. It's one of the most sought-after experiences in the park.

⑥ Rock 'n' Roller Coaster® Starring Aerosmith

A sign warns "prepare to merge as you've never merged before," but by then it's far too late. Your limo zooms from 0 to 60 mph (97 km/h) in 2.8 seconds and into multiple inversions as Aerosmith **(above)** blares at 32,000 watts.

⑧ Fantasmic!

Lasers, fireworks, waterborne images **(below)**, Disney tunes, and a sorcerer mouse are the stars of this end-of-the-day extravaganza *(see p99)* that pits the forces of good against Disney villains such as Maleficent and Cruella de Vil. Performance times vary seasonally.

Disney's Hollywood Studios®

⑦ Twilight Zone Tower of Terror™

The spooky surroundings are but a facade hiding the real terror, a gut-tightening, 13-story fall. Many consider it Disney's best thrill ride.

TOP 10 ⭐ Disney's Animal Kingdom® Park

As the name implies, wildlife rules at the fourth and largest of Disney's parks, which is home to 300 species of animals and birds spread across 500 acres (2 sq km) of lush landscape. Here, the serious issue of conservation is combined with the playfulness of a theme park. Visitors can take a safari and observe tigers in Asia, gorillas in Africa, and elephants, giraffes, hippos and rhinos from a distance. The center of the park has the meticulously carved Tree of Life, which lights up at dusk.

Kilimanjaro Safaris® ①

The park's most popular ride (right) puts riders on a large safari jeep to bump along dirt tracks through the savanna in search of black rhinos, lions, and zebras. While most active early in the morning, they are just as visible during the park's evening safaris, when nocturnal activities offer a different view of the savanna.

② Expedition Everest

In this thrill-filled adventure, your train ascends the snowcapped mountain, before coming to an abrupt stop at a tangled track. You're then sent careening backward in complete darkness, twisting and turning through caverns and canyons, with the legendary Yeti lurking in the shadows. You must be 44 inches (112 cm) to ride.

③ Pangani Forest Exploration Trail®

As you're surrounded by thick vegetation, it's sometimes hard to see the animals on this walk in the woods with a difference. The gorillas (left) are the main attraction, but if the stars of the show prove shy, you can also spot hippos, exotic birds, and weird-looking mole-rats.

Disney's Animal Kingdom® Park

 Festival of The Lion King
One of Orlando's best shows **(above)** won't fail to throw you into the spirit of things. This production uses singers, dancers, and *The Lion King*'s popular score to emphasize nature's diversity.

NEED TO KNOW

MAP G1 ■ Savannah Circle ■ 407-824-4321 ■ www.disneyworld.com

Open 8am–8:30pm, with extended seasonal hours

Adm (1-day ticket, park-specific): adults $116–137; children (3–9) $110–132 (incl tax); under-3s go free

Kali River Rapids®: ages 8 and over

DINOSAUR: ages 9 and over

The Boneyard®: for children aged 3–12

■ The best times to see the animals are at opening time and within an hour of closing.

■ Make FastPass+ *(see p140)* reservations ahead.

Park Guide

Maps are available at the park entrance. After-dark experiences include the Tree of Life Awakenings, and Rivers of Light, plus street celebrations with music and dancers. Pandora – The World of Avatar also brings the spectacular bioluminescent landscapes to life at night.

7 The Boneyard®
Possibly the best playground in any of the parks, this dinosaur dig site is perfect for kids to burn off surplus energy – it is educational and fun.

8 Pandora – The World of Avatar
See floating mountains, trees, and the Valley of Mo'ara during the day, and enjoy the glowing lights at night in this fantasy world. Do not miss the Flight of Passage and Na'Vi River Journey rides.

9 Finding Nemo – The Musical
The Theater in the Wild® is transformed into an enchanted undersea world for this original 30-minute stage show, which merges puppetry with live performances.

5 DINOSAUR
Expect to be shaken up on this ride, which takes you back 65 million years. Convincing animatronic dinosaurs lurk in the darkness. You need to be 40 inches (102 cm) to ride.

6 It's Tough to Be a Bug!®
Located inside the Tree of Life's 50-ft (15-m) base, this 3-D, effect-filled show offers a view of the world from an insect's perspective.

10 Kali River Rapids®
The park's conservation message is evident on this raft ride **(right)**, which passes from a lush landscape to one in the process of being scorched for logging. You need to be 38 inches (96 cm) tall to ride, and you will get wet.

TOP 10 ⭐ Universal Studios Florida™

Universal's first Florida park opened in 1990, with studio-themed attractions and rides based on blockbusters ranging from Hollywood classics to TV favorites. While once a mere distraction from the Mouse, its attractions based on much-loved brands, TV shows and movie characters have seen Universal Studios Florida™ become a vacation destination in its own right.

4 Despicable Me Minion Mayhem

Explore the lair and secret lab of super-villain Gru in this interactive 3-D digital adventure. Riders are transformed into Minions and taken to a Minion dance party.

5 E.T. Adventure®

Everyone's favorite alien takes guests on a bike ride to save his planet. Pedal through strange landscapes to meet Tickli Moot Moot and other characters created by Steven Spielberg especially for this ride.

1 The Simpsons Ride™

Swoop, soar, and smash your way through Krustyland **(above)** on a motion simulator ride with Bart and the rest of this top US cartoon family.

2 Hollywood Rip Ride Rockit®

Choose your own sound-track on this 65-mph (105 km/h) coaster **(below)**, which towers 17 stories above Universal, spills into CityWalk™, and has a record-breaking loop.

Universal Studios Florida™

San Francisco ❸
❻ New York ❼
❿ World Expo
❾ Hollywood ❶
❹ Production Central Woody Woodpecker's KidZone ❺
❷ ❽
Entrance

3 Fast & Furious: Supercharged™

Feel your heart pound as you ride this full-throttle, high-octane vehicles alongside Dom, Letty, Hobbs, and the rest of the *Fast & Furious* crew.

6 Revenge of The Mummy®

This high-speed coaster propels riders backward and forward through ancient Egyptian tombs to face their deepest fears, heightened by darkness, as Imhotep unleashes his wrath.

Previous pages Universal Globe outside the entrance to Universal Studios Florida™

8 Woody Woodpecker's Nuthouse Coaster®

Like the Barnstormer in Disney's Magic Kingdom® *(see p51)*, this 55-second ride for the young (and timid adults) has just one corkscrew.

9 Shrek 4-D

See, hear, and feel the action in "OgreVision" as Shrek and Donkey go to rescue Princess Fiona from Lord Farquaad.

10 Transformers: The Ride-3D

Be a part of the smashing, explosive action of this thrilling ride **(above)**, based on the popular movies, which includes 60-ft (18-m) tall 3-D robots.

7 MEN IN BLACK™ Alien Attack™

You and your "alienator" must keep the intergalactic bad guys from taking over the world as you spin through the streets, looking to shoot the monstrous bugs **(above)**.

NEED TO KNOW

MAP T1 ■ 1000 Universal Studios Plaza ■ 407-363-8000 ■ www.universal orlando.com

Open 9am–6pm, with extended seasonal hours

Adm (1-day ticket): adults $115–129; children (3–9) $108–119; under-3s go free

The Simpsons Ride™ and *Despicable Me*: min height 40 inches (102 cm)

MEN IN BLACK™ Alien Attack™: min height 42 inches (107 cm)

Hollywood Rip Ride Rockit®: min height 51 inches (130 cm)

Revenge of the Mummy®: min height 48 inches (122 cm)

■ You can buy the Universal Express™ Pass *(see p140)* that helps reduce wait times.

■ VIP tours *(see p141)* help beat the crowds during peak periods.

Park Guide

It takes about 20 minutes to get from the parking lot to the attractions. If you're staying at a Universal hotel, use the early admission perk; otherwise, arrive early and hit the major rides first. The on-site hotels offer complimentary transportation to the parks.

Shows and Kids' Stuff

 Beat Builders
Members of construction crews put on impromptu percussion shows in the midst of their work, using everything from buckets and scaffolding to wrench xylophones.

 Universal's Cinematic Celebration™
This lagoon show lights up the night with a celebration of music from the famous and biggest movies of the world, along with a water-and-light spectacle.

③ Animal Actors on Location
This creative animal show features wild, wacky, and occasionally weird live and video animal action. Expect plenty of audience participation.

④ Fear Factor Live
Do you have the nerve to star in this extreme audience participation show? Perform all kinds of stunts as you compete against other guests. Unscripted and unpredictable.

⑤ Curious George Goes To Town
Follow in the footsteps of the mischievous monkey Curious George at this interactive playground, which offers water-based fun and an arena with thousands of soft sponge balls.

The Blues Brothers® live show

⑥ The Blues Brothers®
Fans of the movie, which starred John Belushi and Dan Ackroyd in the key roles, will enjoy this foot-stomping 20-minute revue.

⑦ Kang and Kodos Twirl 'n' Hurl
This kid-friendly *Simpsons*-inspired ride (unlike its name) takes riders gently up and down while spinning round. Think Dumbo the Flying Elephant at the Magic Kingdom® *(see p51)*, but with an edgy twist.

⑧ Universal's Superstar Parade™
Themed floats, street performers, and larger-than-life characters – including Spongebob Squarepants, Dora and Diego, Gru, Agnes, Edith, Margo, and the Minions – get the party started through the streets of Universal Studios Florida™.

⑨ A Day in the Park with Barney™
The puffy purple dinosaur is adored by preschool kids, so this 25-minute sing-along show is guaranteed to get small fans into a frenzy. Everyone else should probably steer clear.

⑩ Universal Orlando's Horror Makeup Show™
A hilarious and educational look at special effects makeup used in the movies. Universal unveils the industry secrets with movie clips, props, and demonstrations.

Curious George Goes To Town

BEHIND THE SCENES

Universal Studios Florida™ is more than just a tourist attraction. Since opening in 1990, it has also been the production site for thousands of television shows, commercials, music videos, and movies. While TV and movie production has been scaled back in favor of theme park rides and live entertainment (such as Blue Man Group at Universal CityWalk™), there are still six sound stages, two event stages, broadcast studios, casting and makeup services, post-production editing facilities, and various backlot film sets, including re-creations of New York City streets, Hollywood Boulevard, and many others. Though these areas are not normally open to the public, if park guests want to be part of some camera action, they can join the studio audience when TV shows shoot episodes at Universal. Tickets for these productions are typically distributed free of charge on the day of taping. Visitors can check in advance with Guest Services to find out if special-event TV shows will be taped during their visit. There are also regular presentations that give a behind-the-scenes look at the movie-making process.

Bart Simpson at Universal

TOP 10 MOVIES MADE AT UNIVERSAL STUDIOS FLORIDA™

1 *Psycho IV* (1990)

2 *The Waterboy* (1998)

3 *Hoover* (1998)

4 *House on Haunted Hill* (1999)

5 *Beethoven's Big Break* (2008)

6 *Ace Ventura Jr* (2009)

7 *The Final Destination* (2009)

8 *The Renee Project* (2011)

9 *Tooth Fairy 2* (2011)

10 *Sharknado 3* (2015)

Star Spotting
Universal Studios Florida™ doesn't just allow you to "ride the movies." Here, you get to meet the stars, too. Actors playing silver-screen and TV legends can be seen around the park and are always willing to pose for photos.

Hollywood Boulevard set at Universal Studios Florida™

TOP 10 ⭐ Universal's Islands of Adventure™

Orlando didn't have a lot to offer adrenaline junkies until Universal unveiled its second Central Florida park in 1999. Universal's Islands of Adventure™ brought immersive settings filled with thrilling attractions, including terrifying roller coasters and heart-stopping water rides. Its stunningly creative experiences seem to jump right out of the screen or the pages of a storybook.

1 Dudley Do-Right's Ripsaw Falls®

Expect to get wet on this thrilling flume ride **(right)**. Dudley's adventure peaks with a 75-ft (23-m) drop at speeds reaching 50 mph (80 km/h) – you'll then plummet some 15 ft (4.5 m) below the water's surface (albeit safely behind glass) before the ride's end.

2 Pteranodon Flyers®

Eye-catching metal gondolas swing from side to side on this prehistoric bird's-eye tour around the Jurassic Park zone.

3 The Amazing Adventures of Spider-Man®

Slap on 3-D glasses and battle the baddies while fireballs and other high-definition objects fly at you. The experience is truly amazing **(below)**.

4 Doctor Doom's Fearfall®

You'll climb 200 ft (61 m), before free-falling and stalling, and then falling again – a sequence repeated to thrilling effect.

Universal's Islands of Adventure™

Poseidon's Fury® ⑤

The line takes you through dark, eerie ruins **(right)** setting the scene for the special effects show. A thrilling 42-ft (13-m) vortex of water forms a projection screen for the epic battle between the titans – Poseidon and Lord Darkenon.

Incredible Hulk Coaster® ⑧

One of the biggest thrills in the park, especially since its revamp. Blast out of the darkness at up to 67 mph (108 km/h), go weightless, and endure inversions and drops.

Skull Island: Reign of Kong ⑩

Vehicles take you deep into the ruins of Skull Island for an intense encounter with fierce beasts, prehistoric predators, gigantic bugs, and Kong himself.

Popeye & Bluto's Bilge-Rat Barges ⑨

Another – less intense – water ride **(right)**, this time aboard a 12-person raft going through white-water rapids. It is also targeted by a number of water cannons.

Jurassic Park River Adventure® ⑥

This ride may start slowly, but it picks up speed as raptors get loose. To escape you'll have to take the 85-ft (26-m) flume-style plunge.

The Cat in the Hat™ ⑦

Hold on as your couch spins and turns through 18 Seussian scenes. The Cat, Thing One, and Thing Two join you on a ride through a day that's anything but ordinary.

NEED TO KNOW

MAP T1 ■ Hollywood Way ■ 407-363-8000 ■ www.universalorlando.com

Open at least 9am–6pm, with extended seasonal hours

Adm (1-day ticket, park specific): adults $115–129; children (3–9) $108–119; under-3s go free

Incredible Hulk Coaster®: min height 54 inches (137 cm)

The Amazing Adventures of Spider-Man®: min height 40 inches (102 cm)

Doctor Doom's Fearfall®: min height 52 inches (132 cm)

Pteranodon Flyers®: height 36–56 inches (91–142 cm); if taller, must accompany a rider of that height

Jurassic Park River Adventure®: min height 42 inches (107 cm)

■ 1-day tickets can be upgraded to a 2-day pass.

■ The Universal Express™ Pass (*see p140*) cuts waiting times.

■ VIP tours (*see p141*) are also available.

Park Guide

It can take 20 minutes to get to the park from the parking lot. Arrive early; anyone staying at a Universal resort can enter before other visitors. Guests at the Royal Pacific, Hard Rock, and Loews Portofino Bay Hotel also get free Universal Express Access (otherwise from $39.99).

Gentler Attractions

1 Jurassic Park® Discovery Center
See through a dinosaur's eyes, match your DNA to theirs, and watch an animatronic velociraptor "hatch" in the laboratory. There are several interactive stations, where kids can brush up on their dinosaur facts.

2 Caro-Seuss-el™
This merry-go-round replaces the traditional horses with versions of Dr. Seuss's cowfish, elephant birds, and mulligatawnies. Regular carousels will never seem quite the same again.

3 If I Ran the Zoo™
The 19 interactive stations in this Seussian playground include flying water snakes, caves, and water cannons, as well as a place to tickle the toes of a Seussian critter.

4 Flight of the Hippogriff™
This family-friendly roller coaster dives into the Forbidden Forest, and then weaves its way past the pumpkin patch and Hagrid's hut.

5 One Fish, Two Fish, Red Fish, Blue Fish™
Fly your fish up, down, and all around on an aerial carousel ride just 15 ft (4 m) off the ground. If you don't do what the song says, you'll get sprayed with water.

One Fish, Two Fish, Red Fish, Blue Fish™

High in the Sky Seuss Trolley Train Ride!

6 High in the Sky Seuss Trolley Train Ride!™
Follow the story of the Sneetches™ on this gentle ride above the attractions of Seuss Landing.

7 Camp Jurassic™
Burn off energy in an adventure playground full of places to explore, including dark caves where "spitters" (small dinosaurs) lurk. See if you can find out how to make the dinosaurs roar.

8 Me Ship, The Olive®
The play area here is full of interactive fun, while Cargo Crane offers an alternative hands-on experience: a chance to fire water cannons at riders on Popeye & Bluto's Bilge-Rat Barges (see p31).

9 The Mystic Fountain
Make a wish at this fountain in Sinbad's Village. This wonderful fountain is surprisingly playful, asking questions of and teasing guests. Don't stand too close or the fountain will spray you.

10 Storm Force Accelatron®
Dizziness is the name of the game as you and X-Men superhero Storm spin your vehicle fast enough to create enough electrical energy to send the villainous Magneto to the great beyond.

IOA'S "STATE-OF-THE-FUTURE" RIDES

The Incredible Hulk

Guests at Universal's Islands of Adventure™ get a first-hand demonstration of some of the most technologically advanced attractions ever created. The Amazing Adventures of Spider-Man® (see p30) took 5 years and more than $100 million to develop. New digital film technologies had to be invented for the floor-to-ceiling 3-D images projected to a moving audience. The motion simulator, wind cannons, and pyrotechnics are all synchronized by a vast computer network. For the immersive experience of Reign of Kong (see p31), screens create a seamless tunnel of realistic 3-D imagery across the high-tech vehicles, which together with next-generation technology puts riders right in the middle of the action. Unique to the Incredible Hulk Coaster (see p31) is a thrust system that catapults the sleek cars out of a specially designed tunnel rather than the usual long, slow haul to the top of an incline. Even so, some low-tech touches can't be avoided: just below is a huge net to catch the belongings that fall from screaming riders.

TOP 10 FACTS

1 Steven Spielberg produced the films shown in The Amazing Adventures of Spider-Man®.

2 Spider-Man's screens are up to 90 ft (27 m) wide.

3 The shock in Spider-Man is a frequency low enough to make humans sick.

4 The Spider-Man ride actually only moves 12 inches (30 cm) up or down.

5 The 40-ft (12-m) vehicle in Skull Island: Reign of Kong weighs 17 tons.

6 The trackless ride uses a positioning system.

7 Wheels are steered individually for maneuvers.

8 The Incredible Hulk Coaster®'s car design is inspired by military aircraft.

9 The Hulk is 3,700 ft (1.1 km) long and can take 1,920 riders per hour.

10 The Hulk's G-force is the same as that of an F-16 fighter jet attack.

The Amazing Adventures of Spider-Man® treats riders to zero-gravity inversions as they are spun upside down at 110 ft (33 m) above the ground, before dropping 105 ft (32 m) at a speed of more than 60 mph (96 km/h).

TOP 10 ⭐ The Wizarding World of Harry Potter™

Bringing to life the magical world from the pages of J.K. Rowling's books and the big screen, Universal's Wizarding World of Harry Potter™ is in two parks – Universal's Islands of Adventure™ and Universal Studios Florida™, connected by the Hogwarts™ Express. Meticulously detailed streetscapes and immersive rides combine to create the magical village of Hogsmeade™ and Diagon Alley™ shopping district. Whether touring Hogwarts Castle or dodging fire-breathing dragons in Gringotts™ bank, the spell of Harry Potter has been cast.

Shopping in Diagon Alley™ **1**

Pick up Quidditch equipment, robes, chocolate frogs, even extendable ears from an array of shops here **(right)**, including Weasleys' Wizard Wheezes™. Turn into *(see p107)* Knockturn Alley for darker objects at Borgin and Burkes™.

2 Harry Potter and the Escape from Gringotts™

Even the line for this thrill ride through the underground vaults of Gringotts™ bank is breathtaking – you enter through a grand lobby of diligently working goblins. The ride itself combines coaster and simulator as you evade the bank's security, not to mention Bellatrix and Voldemort. Note that this is the only ride in Diagon Alley™.

Diagon Alley™

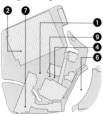

3 Flight of the Hippogriff™

This family-friendly coaster introduces you to the Hippogriff and takes you on a training flight around the pumpkin patch and Hagrid's Hut.

4 Spell Casting – Interactive Wand Experiences

Interactive wands are on sale at Ollivanders™, and produce various effects when swished or flicked at locations marked on the included map.

5 Harry Potter and the Forbidden Journey™

The line takes you on a tour through Hogwarts, before you soar over the grounds in this simulator ride. Riders get tossed around, and come face to face with Dementors.

6 The Knight Bus™

Parked just outside Diagon Alley™ is the purple triple-decker Knight Bus™, where you chat with the conductor.

Hogsmeade™

8 The Nighttime Lights At Hogwarts™ Castle

Hogsmeade™ village **(below)** comes to life with a dazzling spectacle of special effects, music, and lights in a celebration of the four houses of Hogwarts. At nightfall, watch the spirit of each house wrap itself around the castle.

NEED TO KNOW

MAP T1 ■ Hogsmeade™: Universal's Islands of Adventure™; Diagon Alley™: Universal Studios Florida™ ■ 407-363-8000 ■ www.universal orlando.com

Open 9am–6pm, with extended seasonal hours

Adm (1-day ticket to both parks): adult $170–184; children (3–9) $165–179; under-3s free

■ Sample some frothy, creamy, and very tasty Butterbeer (served cold, warm, or frozen) at the Three Broomsticks, the Leaky Cauldron, or a quick-stop cart.

■ Overseen by a goblin, Gringotts™ Money Exchange will swap your Muggle currency for Gringotts™ Bank Notes. These are treated as cash through out Universal Orlando Resort™. You may want to hold onto a few notes to keep as your souvenirs.

Park Guide
The Universal Express™ Pass offers access to all the rides and attractions at Wizarding World of Harry Potter™, including Hogwarts™ Express.

9 Street Performances

In Diagon Alley™ there are live singers and puppet shows based on *The Tales of Beedle the Bard*. Hogsmeade™ show-cases the Frog Choir, while Durmstrang and Beauxbatons students perform in the Triwizard Spirit Rally at Hogwarts.

7 Hogwarts™ Express

With regular departures from both King's Cross and Hogsmeade™ stations, guests with multi-park passes can travel between parks aboard this steam train **(below)**. Once the doors close on your compart-ment, you'll whiz through the English countryside; Ron, Hermione, and Harry are on board, too.

10 Ollivanders™

The wand chooses the wizard at this inter-active experience – and it only chooses one. Both Ollivanders™ wand shops are spectacular, but Diagon Alley's is bigger, and therefore boasts shorter lines.

TOP 10 ⭐ LEGOLAND®

This kid-friendly theme park opened in 2011, to the delight of children aged 2–12 and their parents. Like its counterparts around the world, it boasts larger-than-life LEGO® creations (along with thousands of smaller models), and more than 50 LEGO®- and DUPLO®- based rides, shows, and attractions. Kids can fly, drive, build, and climb their way through miniature cities, medieval kingdoms, and ancient Egyptian ruins. In addition, the beautiful Botanical Gardens, which predate both the theme park and next-door Water Park, are well worth visiting.

① The Great LEGO® Race
In this rollicking race set in a virtual world, compete against a number of LEGO® mini-figures while riding a roller-coaster. Experience the action from every direction – up, down, forward, and backward.

④ Imagination Zone
Filled with hands-on activities that encourage creativity **(right)**, here kids can design their own cutting-edge robots, play the latest LEGO® video games, or build their own creations with real or virtual LEGO® blocks.

② The Dragon
Ride high above the park's version of a medieval village in a dragon-themed coaster **(above)**, twisting and turning both indoors and out, along a track that winds its way through the enchanted LEGOLAND® Castle.

⑤ DUPLO® Valley
Little children can board the DUPLO Train to explore the country-side, look for missing farm animals on the DUPLO Tractor ride, cool off in the DUPLO Splash and Play area, or climb around in the DUPLO Farm play area.

⑥ LEGOLAND® Water Park
Located next to the theme park (and ticketed separately), LEGOLAND® Water Park offers plenty of soggy attractions for cooling off on a hot day, including a wave pool, lazy river, and numerous splash and play areas.

Botanical Gardens ③
First planted in 1936, these exotic gardens **(right)** were preserved as part of the building works at LEGOLAND®. See an array of plants, including a huge banyan tree.

7 Flying School
With their feet dangling freely, riders will seemingly fly through the air (or at least along the track) on this suspended roller coaster ride. The Flying School opens later than the park in the morning on select dates throughout the year.

9 Pirate's Cove Live Water Ski Show
This 20-minute live-action show entertains the crowds with water-skiers, jet-skiers, boats, and pyrotechnic special effects, as guards seek to protect the ship *Brickbeard's Bounty* from marauding pirates.

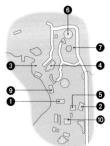

LEGOLAND®

10 LEGO® Movies in 4-D
A variety of 4-D productions, including a special NEXO Knights movie and *The LEGO® Movie* (below), are shown in a 700-seat theater. Kids will love the multi-sensory movies, while parents will enjoy a few minutes off their feet. After the show, characters meet and greet outside the theater.

8 Larger than Life LEGO® Creations
Dotted around the theme park are a number of LEGO® models, some over 6 ft (1.8 m) tall, and all built block by block. Look out for replicas of famous Florida sights, Las Vegas, and scenes from Star Wars.

NEED TO KNOW

MAP B2 ■ 1 Legoland Way, Winter Haven ■ 877-350-5346 ■ www.LEGOLAND.com/florida

Open most days 10am–6pm in season; closed Tuesdays and Wednesdays during select seasons; Water Park closes for most of the fall and winter seasons

Adm (1-day ticket, park specific): adults $93.99; children (3–9) $88.99; under-3s go free; multi-day and multi-park tickets are available

■ Weekends bring larger crowds and in the hot weather that means the Water Park gets very busy.

■ The LEGOLAND® Hotel and LEGOLAND® Beach Retreat, with themed rooms and suites, are ideally located for visitors.

Park Guide

On entering the park, pick up a map and show guide at Guest Services. Check show times, character meet and greets, and operating hours of the rides to ensure you can fit everything into your time at the park.

TOP 10 ⭐ Merritt Island

Thanks to the US government's race into space, Merritt Island National Wildlife Refuge at the Kennedy Space Center Visitor Complex has become the second-largest reserve in Florida. Founded in 1963 to serve as a security buffer zone for NASA, its 219 sq miles (567 sq km) now provide an important habitat for endangered species and a vital stopover along the migration path of hundreds of birds. The manatees are the refuge's most popular attraction.

5 Manatee Observation Deck

Most common in spring and fall, manatees frequent the refuge year-round. See them up close in Banana River or from the viewing platform at Haulover Canal.

1 Boating
Boating or canoeing **(above)** is still the best way to get close to the wildlife. In season, the waterways are filled with wading birds at migratory pit stops and manatees in the depths.

2 Fishing
With both Florida State and Refuge fishing permits, you can cast your line on the Indian River, Banana River, and Mosquito Lagoon. Red drum, spotted sea trout, and snook are the most common catches.

3 Visitor Center
In addition to a 20-minute video, the center has exhibits and educational displays providing a good introduction to the Island. The ponds behind the center are favorite spots for alligators.

4 Black Point Wildlife Drive
The best places to spot wildlife here are linked by an easy access drive. Follow the 7-mile (11-km), one-way loop to see a variety of waterfowl, wading birds, and raptors.

6 Bird Tours
The reserve organizes birdwatching tours for beginners, where park volunteers will help you identify many of the different species **(below)** in the refuge.

NEED TO KNOW

MAP A3 ■ East of Titusville on SR 402 ■ 321-861-0667 ■ www.fws.gov/refuge/merritt_island

Open Nov–Mar: 9am–4pm daily; Apr–Oct 9am–4pm Mon–Sat; closed on federal holidays

Adm $10 per vehicle

Visitor Center: 4 miles (6.4 km) farther along SR 406

■ Grab a bite to eat at the friendly, casual Dixie Crossroads, a few miles up the road in Titusville.

■ The best times to go on the Black Point Wildlife Drive are 1–2 hours after sunrise and before sunset.

■ Birdwatching is best from October through April. Alligators can be encountered at any time – be extremely cautious when viewing them.

■ From 1-95, take exit 220 and head east for four miles on SR 402 (Garden Street).

Audio Guide

The visitor center has audio guides for the Black Point Wildlife Drive, and you can also pick up a self-guided brochure near the drive entrance. This provides info on the best places to spot wildlife along the route.

8 Hiking

There are seven hiking trails (left) on offer. Most are quite wet, but none are too strenuous. They range from a quarter of a mile (0.4 km) to 5 miles (8 km).

9 Beaches

Visitors to the refuge spend more time on land than in water, but Playalinda Beach provides access, parking, and other facilities for swimmers. Beware of alligators on the road to the beach.

7 Waterfowl Hunting

So large are the numbers of birds involved in the seasonal migration that hunting for ducks and coot is allowed from November to January. Permits and safety cards are required, and trips must return by early afternoon.

Merritt Island

10 Migrations

All year round, the refuge plays host to migrating animals. The birds return in May, and in June and July turtles lay eggs on the beaches. Waterfowl abound on rivers in September.

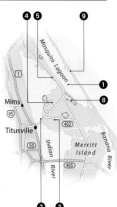

TOP 10 ⭐ Kennedy Space Center Visitor Complex

The Kennedy Space Center Visitor Complex highlights and celebrates the fruits of human inquiry and imagination. Built in 1967, the center has become one of Florida's most popular tourist destinations. Each year, it offers a window on life beyond Earth to more than 1.5 million visitors, and continues to be the site of many spacecraft launches.

1 Apollo/Saturn V Center

Visitors can relive the historic launch of Apollo 8 **(above)** in the Firing Room Theater, and get to walk underneath one of only three Saturn V (see p42) rockets left in existence.

2 Eyes on the Universe

This 20-minute live presentation takes the audience back in time as they look through the lens of the Hubble Space Telescope, exploring the far reaches of the universe in search of answers to questions about the cosmos.

4 Rocket Garden

Unlike any other garden you have seen, this area **(above)** houses eight real spacecraft, including a Mercury Atlas like the one used to launch astronaut John Glenn. Red, white, and blue lighting adds drama to these historic rockets.

5 Heroes & Legends

Experience the dawn of the Space Age and meet the heroes in the U.S. Astronaut Hall of Fame. Visitors can journey through space and time in a 4D theater, and get a close-up view of the Gemini 9 capsule.

Shuttle Launch Experience 3

This exciting simulation ride **(right)** allows all visitors to the Center to experience the unique sights, sounds, and sensations of a space shuttle launch.

(8) KSC Explore Tours

Visitors are treated to an insider's view of the center. Drive by launch pads and disembark for photos at the picturesque NASA Causeway and Vehicle Assembly Building.

(6) Journey to Mars

This attraction combines a live presentation with multimedia exhibits and simulators **(above)** – a reminder that the future of space exploration relies on humanity's drive and innovation.

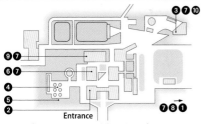

Kennedy Space Center Visitor Complex

(7) Cosmic Quest

Purchase a 1-day badge and it's game on. This live action gaming experience allows players to experience four different immersive astronaut adventures alongside Robonaut, a dexterous humanoid robot.

(9) IMAX – Science on a Sphere

The Center's twin, back-to-back, 5.5-story theaters show two movies: *Journey to Space*, which explores NASA's plans for deep space exploration, and *A Beautiful Planet*, showing stunning images of the Earth's surface.

NEED TO KNOW

MAP B3 ■ Rte 405, Titusville ■ 877-313-2610 ■ www.kennedy spacecenter.com

Open 9am–6pm daily

Adm adults $57, children (3–11) $47, under-3s free

....

■ Rocket launch tickets must be purchased in advance. Call 877-313-2610 for information on launch viewing tickets.

■ Call for tour details.

■ Grab a hot dog and sit next to a piece of real moon rock at the Moon Rock Café.

■ Gray Line Orlando provides tickets and transportation to the Visitor Complex with stops in Orlando and Kissimmee. Call 407-522-5911 or visit www.graylineorlando.com

Center Guide

About a 55-minute drive from Orlando, the Center is within the Merritt Island National Wildlife Refuge *(see pp38–9)*. Admission includes a bus tour with a view of a launch pad and the Apollo 8 launch site, ending at the Apollo/Saturn V Center. Board the bus tour inside the complex, through the information center; rent a KSC SmartGuide. Except for launch days, the center is rarely overcrowded.

(10) Space Shuttle Atlantis

Admire a close-up view of the Atlantis displayed here in mid-flight glory. There are more than 60 interactive exhibits.

Rockets: Past, Present, and Future

 Jupiter C
This early variation of the Mercury Redstone rocket was developed by a team headed by the German scientist Wernher von Braun. The Jupiter C carried the USA's first satellite, Explorer I, which launched on January 31, 1958.

Neil A. Armstrong and the X-15

2 X-15
The X-15 rocket plane flew 199 missions from 1959 to 1968, carrying a who's who of astronauts, including moon-walker Neil Armstrong. It reached altitudes of 354,200 ft (107,960 m) and speeds of 4,520 mph (7,274 km/h).

3 Mercury Redstone
This rocket carried the first American into space. Alan B. Shepard Jr.'s 15-minute, 22-second ride aboard the Freedom 7 capsule in 1961 was one of six flights in the Mercury program.

4 Mercury Atlas
When the six-flight Mercury program graduated from sub-orbital to orbital flights, the Atlas replaced the Mercury Redstone. It was this rocket that took John H. Glenn Jr., Scott Carpenter, Wally Schirra, and Gordon Cooper into space in 1962 and 1963.

5 Titan II
When a larger capsule was needed for two-person crews, this rocket earned its place in NASA history. It was used for a total of 10 manned flights (Gemini Titan expeditions) in 1965 and 1966.

6 Saturn 1B
The Saturn 1B launched Apollo lunar spacecraft into Earth's orbit in the mid-1960s, in training for manned flights to the moon. Later, it launched three missions to man the Skylab space station (1973), as well as the American crew for the Apollo/Soyuz Test Project (1975).

7 Saturn V
At 363 ft (110 m), this was the largest launch vehicle ever produced. The highlight of its career was Apollo 11, the 3-astronaut mission that famously landed Buzz Aldrin and Neil Armstrong on the moon on July 20, 1969.

8 Titan Centaur
The Titan Centaur rocket launched Voyager I and II in 1977, on a mission to explore Jupiter, Saturn, Uranus, and – 12 years after its launch – Neptune.

9 Pegasus
Today's version of this winged wonder is capable of flying small communications satellites into a low Earth orbit from the bellies of mother ships, such as the L-1011.

10 X-43A Launch Vehicle
These diminutive scramjet aircraft may one day be able to boost small, unmanned jets at high speeds and altitudes, thereby vastly improving the safety of manned flights.

Mercury Redstone

THE SPACE SHUTTLE

Space Shuttle at the Visitor Complex

The space shuttles were the first fully reusable spacecraft and the best recognized of NASA's vehicles. Five of them ventured into space: Columbia, Challenger, Discovery, Atlantis, and Endeavour. Once in orbit, the shuttles were capable of cruising at 17,500 mph (28,163 km/h), and their cargo bays could hold a fully loaded tour bus, yet the engineless orbiters could glide to a runway more gracefully than a pelican landing on water. Despite the loss of two of the space-craft and their crews – Challenger in 1986 and Columbia in 2003 – the shuttles were a remarkable success. They were pivotal in building the International Space Station and extending the life of the Hubble Space Telescope, and their crews carried out valuable cutting-edge research while in orbit.

TOP 10
US CREWED SPACE PROGRAM EVENTS

1 May 5, 1961 Alan B. Shepard Jr. becomes the first American in space.

2 Feb 20, 1962 John H. Glenn Jr. becomes the first American to orbit the Earth.

3 Jun 3, 1965 Edward H. White Jr. becomes the first American to walk in space.

4 Jul 20, 1969 Neil Armstrong becomes the first person to walk on the moon.

5 Apr 11–13, 1970 An explosion nearly causes disaster for Apollo 13.

6 Apr 12, 1981 The first shuttle is launched.

7 Jan 28, 1986 Seven astronauts die in the Challenger space shuttle explosion.

8 May 27–Jun 6, 1999 The space shuttle docks for the first time on the International Space Station.

9 Feb 1, 2003 Columbia explodes on re-entering Earth's atmosphere, killing seven astronauts.

10 Jul 21, 2011 The shuttle program ends with the landing of Endeavour at Kennedy Space Center Visitor Complex.

Columbia was the first space shuttle to launch in 1981. Astronauts John Young and Robert Crippen spent 54 hours in Earth's orbit and landed at Edwards Air Force Base in California. The shuttle completed 26 further missions before disintegrating at the end of its 28th mission.

The Top 10 of Everything

The rip-roaring Incredible Hulk Coaster®

🔟 Museums

Contemporary Figurative Art: Selections from the Orlando Museum of Art

1 Orlando Museum of Art

The Orlando Museum of Art (OMA) is one of the Southeast's top arts museums *(see p119)*. The fine permanent collection is dominated by pre-Columbian art and American artists such as Georgia O'Keefe, George Inness, Dale Chihuly, Robert Rauschenberg, Robin Rhode, Kate Gilmore, and Frederick MacMonnies. These works are supplemented by touring exhibitions from major metropolitan museums, and numerous smaller shows of regional or local significance, although curators tend to avoid overtly controversial works.

2 Orange County Regional History Center

Given the region's relatively short history, this museum *(see p121)* has wisely ignored geographic limitations. Exhibits include local photographs and memorabilia as well as a re-created Victorian parlor, a 1926 fire station, and fascinating temporary shows that cover themes such as pirates and space travel.

3 Mennello Museum of American Art

This small lakeside museum *(see p120)* houses an unusual and charming collection of paintings by obscure curio shop owner and Floridian folk artist Earl Cunningham (1893–1977). In addition to his own work, there are traveling exhibitions that feature the works of other "outsider" artists.

4 Orlando Science Center

This huge, attention-grabbing, exploratorium-style museum *(see p119)* boasts hundreds of interactive, child-friendly exhibits designed to introduce kids to the wonders of science. The center's ten themed zones deal with subjects ranging from mechanics to math, health and fitness to lasers, making this an educational and fun break from the usual theme park distractions. Don't miss the CineDome, which houses a planetarium and the world's largest Iwerks® theater.

Hands on at Orlando Science Center

5 Cornell Fine Arts Museum

Located on the campus of Rollins College, the small, stylish Cornell (see p126) is one of Florida's oldest art collections. It showcases European and American paintings, sculpture, and decorative arts from the Renaissance and Baroque periods to the 20th century. Highlights include *Madonna and Child Enthroned* (c.1480) by Cosimo Rosselli, and *Reclining Figure* (1982) by Henry Moore.

6 Holocaust Memorial Resource & Education Center

MAP J3 ▪ 851 N. Maitland Ave ▪ 407-628-0555 ▪ Open 9am–4pm Mon–Thu (to 1pm Fri), 1–4pm Sun ▪ www.holocaustedu.org

Founded in 1980 by Holocaust survivors and witnesses, the memorial aims to inculcate compassion and generosity in future generations. The museum conducts lectures, hosts a film series, and has a permanent exhibition of remembrances.

7 Charles Hosmer Morse Museum of American Art

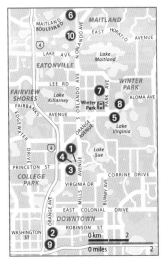

This museum (see p125) displays the world's most comprehensive collection of work by American artist Louis Comfort Tiffany, best known for his Art Nouveau stained glass. Highlights include a chapel made for the 1893 World's Columbian Exposition and a re-creation of Tiffany's New York home.

Loving Cup at Charles Hosmer Morse Museum of American Art

8 Albin Polasek Museum and Sculpture Gardens

Czech-American Polasek (1879–1965) was a figurative sculptor famed for creating a number of landmark public monuments across Chicago. When he retired from his position at the Art Institute of Chicago, he moved to this self-designed house and studio (see p127), where he continued sculpting.

The gardens are filled with his work, as are four galleries in the house, which also hold pieces by other artists.

9 The Grand Bohemian Gallery

MAP D4 ▪ 325 S. Orange Ave ▪ 407-581-4801 ▪ Open 10am–7pm Mon–Sat (to 3pm Sun) ▪ www.grandbohemian gallery.com

The Grand Bohemian Hotel displays over 150 works by local, regional, and internationally acclaimed artists. Pieces include jewelry, ceramics, glassware, and sculpture, as well as paintings.

10 Art & History Museums

MAP J4 ▪ 221 & 231 W. Packwood Ave ▪ 407-539-2181 ▪ Open noon–4pm Thu–Sun ▪ www.artandhistory.org

Artifacts, textiles, and photos from Maitland's pioneer days, including the citrus and lumber industries, are the focus here. The Maitland Art Center is one of the few remainders of Mayan Revival Architecture, while the Telephone Museum has a selection of vintage phones and memorabilia.

Cultural Venues and Organizations

Adventures of Pericles **performance at Orlando Shakes**

① Orlando Shakes
MAP M3 ▪ 812 E. Rollins St ▪ 407-447-1700 ▪ Adm ▪ www.orlandoshakes.org

This nationally recognized theater company performs modern classics and Broadway hits, as well as lots of the Bard's works. Their productions can be seen in an 8-month-long season at their state-of-the-art theater at Loch Haven Park.

② Orlando Repertory Theatre
MAP M3 ▪ 1001 E. Princeton St ▪ 407-896-7365 ▪ Adm

Founded as the Orlando Little Theatre in 1926, the Repertory has evolved into Orlando's only full-time professional theater for young audiences. Broadway performances are offered throughout the year, with past productions including *Junie B. Jones*, Disney's *Little Mermaid*, and *Mary Poppins*.

③ Dr. Phillips Center for the Performing Arts
MAP P3 ▪ 445 S. Magnolia Ave ▪ 844-513-2014 ▪ Adm ▪ www.drphillipscenter.org

This impressive, high-tech hub for the performing arts flaunts two large spaces: the 2,700-seat Walt Disney Theater, used for Broadway traveling shows and other theatrical events, and the 300-seat Alexis & Jim Pugh Theater which boasts a colorful original artwork on the ceiling.

④ Orlando Philharmonic
MAP D4 ▪ 425 N. Bumby Ave ▪ 407-770-0071 ▪ Adm ▪ www.orlandophil.org

Orlando's resident orchestra boasts more than 80 conservatory-trained musicians. Venues vary, but include the Phil's home at The Plaza Live, the Bob Carr Theater, and Dr. Phillips Center for the Performing Arts. It puts on a variety of concert series, from pop to classical and opera.

Orlando Philharmonic orchestra

unjuried music, dance, and other performances, and 100 percent of box office sales go to the artists. It is held at the Lowndes Shakespeare Center, the Orlando Rep, and other nearby sites.

8 Orlando Ballet

MAP M3 ▪ 415 E. Princeton St ▪ 407-426-1733 ▪ Adm ▪ www.orlandoballet.org

This growing company presents four major productions annually, including a version of *The Nutcracker* as well as special performances throughout the year. Smaller shows are held on community stages, with major productions at the Dr. Phillips Center for the Performing Arts.

5 SAK Comedy Lab

MAP P3 ▪ 29 S. Orange Ave ▪ 407-648-0001 ▪ Adm ▪ www.sak.com

A Downtown favorite, SAK is Orlando's home of improvisation comedy. Shows are always funny and inventive, and there are two per night. The 8pm shows are usually family-friendly, while the later ones get a bit edgier, although obscene material is strictly avoided. Of particular interest are the series shows, such as *Foolish Hearts*, an ongoing, improvised soap opera.

6 Enzian Theater

Central Florida's only full-time arthouse cinema *(see p126)* is a unique venue – its single-screen, 250-seat house is arranged like a dinner theater, with wait staff serving food and drinks (including beer and wine). Featuring foreign and American independents, and with regular special-interest festivals, plus the Florida Film Festival *(see p86)*, this is a place for true cinephiles.

7 Orlando International Fringe Festival

The 14-day Orlando Fringe *(see p86)* follows in the footsteps of the grand-daddy of fringe: the Edinburgh Fringe in Scotland. Like Edinburgh, the Orlando Fringe presents uncensored,

Performance at Osceola Arts

9 Osceola Arts

Kissimmee's home of high culture offers a theater, art gallery, and a variety of special events. Osceola Arts *(see p116)* has an engagingly diverse schedule, eagerly offering a little bit of every-thing, from Broadway to barbershop, and storytelling to sculptures.

10 Mad Cow Theatre

MAP P3 ▪ 54 W. Church St ▪ 407-297-8788 ▪ Adm

A favorite among local actors, this mainstay theatrical group has developed a reputation for small but inventive high-quality shows. With a passion for both classic and contemporary productions, the theater presents the best of American and world drama. Past productions have ranged from Chekhov to Neil Simon.

Thrill Rides

1 Rock 'n' Roller Coaster® Starring Aerosmith
This ride *(see p21: Disney's Hollywood Studios®)* accelerates like a military jet. If that isn't enough to make heads spin, each 24-passenger "stretch limo" has 120 speakers that blare Aerosmith hits at a teeth-rattling high volume.

2 Flight of Passage
Discover the beauty and grandeur of the world of Pandora on an exhilarating 3D ride *(see p23: Pandora – The World or Avatar)* aboard a mountain banshee. The breathtaking ride over the incredible landscape of the moon aloows visitors to fly, dip, and soar into the Valley of Mo'ara.

3 Manta®
Headfirst, face-down in a prone position – mimicking the gliding movements of a manta ray, this ride *(see p105: SeaWorld® Orlando)* has its riders soar to the sky, then take a dive, twisting and turning at speeds of up to 60 mph (96 km/h).

4 Hollywood Rip Ride Rockit®
The second tallest (167 ft/51 m) and one of the fastest (65 mph/105 km/h) coasters *(see p26: Universal Studios Florida™)* in Orlando lets you pick a soundtrack before you strap in to a high-tech car. Visitors can buy a recording of the ride to create their own music video later.

Hollywood Rip Ride Rockit®

Riders get soaked at Splash Mountain®

5 Splash Mountain®
Prepare to get drenched on this deep-drop ride *(see p12: Magic Kingdom®)*. In summer, it's a cooling trip; at any time of year it's one to enjoy as a spectator from the bridge between Frontierland® and Adventureland®. Even in that relative safety you may get soaked.

6 Mako
Named after one of the fastest sharks in the ocean, this wild ride *(see p105: SeaWorld® Orlando)* is the fastest (73 mph, 118 km/h), tallest (200 ft/61 m), and longest (2,760 ft/841 m) in Orlando. Putting the hype in this hypercoaster is a feeling of near weightlessness known as "air time," as you speed through the reef, hunting for prey.

7 Incredible Hulk Coaster®
Possibly the ultimate inversion ride, this is a zero-G-force, multi-looping coaster *(see p31: Universal's Islands of Adventure™)*. Recent enhancements add a new storyline – as you wait in line, audio-visuals set you in the middle of an experiment gone wrong.

8 Kraken®
Think pure speed as Poseidon's mythological under-water beast breaks free and without warning pulls your 32-passenger train 151 ft (46 m) closer to the sky, then dives 144 ft (44 m) back toward the ground at speeds of 65 mph (105 km/h). After this descent, expect seven loops on a 4,177-ft (1,273-m) course *(see p105: SeaWorld® Orlando)*. This may just be the longest 3 minutes and 39 seconds of your life.

9 Twilight Zone Tower of Terror™
Take the plunge on the phantom elevator that crosses into the Twilight Zone *(see p21: Disney's Hollywood Studios®)* at the Hollywood Tower Hotel. According to legend, in 1939 five elevator passengers disappeared during a violent thunderstorm, never to be seen again. Not suitable for young children.

Twilight Zone Tower of Terror™

10 Summit Plummet
No water-park slide will tangle up your bathing suit faster than this 120-ft (36-m) partial-darkness ride. It starts slow, but ends in a near vertical drop that has you plummeting at 60 mph (96 km/h). It's not for the weak of heart or those under 48 inches (122 cm).

Entrance to The Cat in the Hat™

TOP 10 THRILL RIDES FOR CHILDREN

1 The Cat in the Hat™
This ride's *(see p31)* dizzying, 24-ft (7-m) tunnel can put your tummy in a spin.

2 Barnstormer
MAP F1 ▪ Magic Kingdom® ▪ Min height 35 in (89cm)
This circus-stunt plane coaster spins its way around the whimsical track.

3 Dumbo
MAP F1 ▪ Magic Kingdom®
Fly round and round, while dipping up and down on this tot-friendly ride.

4 The Magic Carpets of Aladdin
MAP F1 ▪ Magic Kingdom®
A gentle ride aboard a flying carpet.

5 Flight of the Hippogriff™
Like the Barnstormer and Woody's Nuthouse, the corkscrew action of this ride *(see p34)* is a blast.

6 Pteranodon Flyers®
A neat aerial adventure *(see p30)*, but it can make some riders queasy.

7 Peter Pan's Flight
Fly over London and on to Never Land *(see p12)* with Peter and the Lost Boys.

8 Caro-Seuss-el™
Seussian characters make this carousel ride *(see p32)* truly unique.

9 E.T. Adventure®
Pedal your bicycle past fantastic scenery and characters *(see p26)*.

10 Woody Woodpecker's Nuthouse Coaster®
The banked turns of this mini coaster *(see p27)* are absolutely exhilarating.

🔟 Smaller Attractions

Upside-down WonderWorks, packed with hands-on activities

1 WonderWorks

Gimmicks abound inside this building (*see p104*), which is designed to appear as if it is sinking into the ground roof-first. Inside, there is an interactive arcade of some mild scientific educational value. Among more than 85 hands-on activities, the curious can experience an earthquake or virtual hang gliding, and test their reflexes. For simple fun, the huge laser-tag field is a blast.

2 ICON Orlando 360™

At 400 ft (122 m), this observation wheel (*see p106*) is one of the world's tallest. Passengers get a bird's-eye view of the city, which is an impressive sight by day, and even more so by night. Other entertainment options include Madame Tussauds, SKELETONS: Museum of Osteology, and the Orlando StarFlyer, the world's tallest swing ride at 450 ft (137 m). The complex offers more than a dozen restaurants, and bars. There is a central courtyard with choreographed water displays as well as live entertainment, and unique shopping venues. I-Drive itself is laden with small attractions from one end to the other.

3 Ripley's Believe It or Not!® Odditorium

Like WonderWorks, Ripley's (*see p103*) looks like it's about to slip into the ground. You will find squeal-inducing replicas of human and animal oddities, including a two-headed cat. A movie shows people swallowing coat hangers and light bulbs, while quirky displays include a *Mona Lisa* made out of toast.

4 Orlando Watersports Complex

MAP F4 ■ 8615 Florida Rock Rd ■ 407-251-3100 ■ Adm ■ www.aktionparks.com

The complex offers outdoor wake boarding, wake skating, wake surfing and water skiing sessions. Children can splash around at Aquapark, which has slides, climbing towers, and more.

ICON Orlando™ observation wheel

5 iFLY Orlando
Experience sky-diving without jumping from a plane at this vertical wind tunnel *(see p106)*, which has more than 100,000 visitors each year. There are certain weight restrictions and a minimum age of 3, but no experience is necessary. The price covers a class, gear and equipment, and two 1-minute jumps, usually more than enough to exhaust a novice skydiver.

6 Winter Park Scenic Boat Tour
Glide through three of Winter Park's lakes on a pontoon boat during this hour-long tour *(see p125)*. Spot ospreys and herons, or swoon over huge lakeside mansions. The architecture and calm, secluded canals make this tour popular with the kitsch-weary.

Winter Park Scenic Boat Tour

7 Zip Orlando™
Fly over untouched Floridian wilderness, choosing from a range of day or night excursions *(see p113)*. Take a zip-line tour, or opt for the guided ATV tour through the back-country in search of native animals.

8 Reptile World Serpentarium
MAP H6 ▪ 5705 E. Irlo Bronson Memorial Hwy (3.5 miles E. of St Cloud) ▪ 407-892-6905 ▪ Open 10am–5pm Tue–Sun ▪ Adm
This unique, educational, attraction gives visitors the chance to watch a snake handler in action as he extracts poisonous venom from the beasts. It also has the largest reptile exhibit in Florida.

Speedy spins at Fun Spot America

9 Fun Spot America
Looking for life in the fast lane? Fun Spot's *(see p105)* thrilling go-kart tracks and Ferris wheel are complemented by two giant roller coasters and the world's biggest SkyCoaster. For less-adventurous visitors, there are also sedate arcade games and a kid zone.

10 Titanic: The Artifact Exhibition
The spirit of Leonardo DiCaprio lingers around this impressive, 20,000 sq-ft (1858 sq-m) re-creation *(see p105)* of the doomed *Titanic*, which boasts 17 galleries filled with artifacts recovered from the wreckage. Guided tours by actors playing passengers and crew bring the displays to life. There's also an interactive dinner event on Friday and Saturday evenings.

TOP 10 Parks and Preserves

1 Canaveral National Seashore and Merritt Island National Wildlife Refuge

MAP A3 ■ Titusville ■ Seashore park: open 6am–6pm daily ■ Visitor center: open 9am–5pm ■ Refuge: open 9am–4pm; adm ■ Guided tours: www. nps.gov/cana

These federal preserves (see pp38–9) bordering the Kennedy Space Center Visitor Complex are home to endangered sea turtles, manatees, dolphins, alligators, bald eagles, and ospreys. Explore Canaveral's beaches and Merritt's driving routes, trails, and observation deck.

Harry P. Leu Gardens

2 Harry P. Leu Gardens

Wander through sprawling 50-acre botanical gardens (see p119), best seen from October through March. The stunning flora at the formal gardens includes camellias, orchids, azaleas, and 75 varieties of roses. There are gardens devoted to palms, bamboo, and butterflies, too.

3 Bill Frederick Park at Turkey Lake

MAP D3 ■ 3401 S. Hiawassee Rd ■ 407-246-4486 ■ Open 8am–5pm daily (Apr–Oct: to 7pm) ■ Adm

Unlike many more spartan state parks, this 300-acre city retreat has a swimming pool, picnic pavilions, a lake full of fish, nature and jogging trails, three playgrounds, and a farm-animal petting zoo. It also has camping areas.

4 Lake Louisa State Park

MAP B2 ■ State Park Dr, Clermont ■ 352-394-3969 ■ Open 8am–sunset ■ Adm ■ www. floridastateparks.org/lakelouisa

You can fish, swim, or paddle a canoe, but you'll have to bring your own equipment. The beach has a bathhouse with showers, and there's a picnic area. White-tail deer, wild turkeys, marsh rabbits, opossums, and raccoons are common, and a polecat may cut across your path.

5 Lake Eola Park

Enjoy a leisurely stroll along the 0.9-mile (1.4-km) trail that circles the lake here (see p120). Less energetic pursuits include feeding the birds and cruising Lake Eola in the swan-shaped rental boats. The park also hosts seasonal events, including a 4th of July fireworks show. Orlando's farmers' market is held here on Sundays.

Swans at Lake Eola

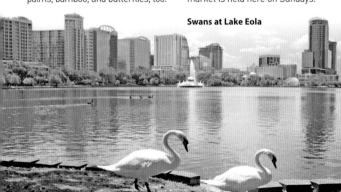

View across Blue Spring State Park

6 Blue Spring State Park

MAP A2 ■ 2100 French Ave, Orange City ■ 366-775-3663 ■ Open 8am–sunset ■ Adm ■ www.floridastateparks.org/park/Blue-Spring

With the largest natural spring on the St. Johns River, Blue Spring is a winter refuge for manatees. Swimmers and snorkelers alike will enjoy the refreshing, crystal-clear waters. Fishing, canoeing, and boating are popular activities here.

7 Disney Wilderness Preserve

MAP H3 ■ 2700 Scrub Jay Trail, Kissimmee ■ 407-935-0002 ■ Open 9am–4:30pm Mon–Fri

The centerpiece of the Everglades Headwaters National Wildlife Refuge and Conservation Center, this Preserve is a center for research on climate change. It is also a great place to hike as it hosts over 1,000 species of flora and fauna – look out for bald eagles, wood storks, sandhill cranes, gopher tortoises, and big-eared bats among the cypress swamps, oak hammocks, and freshwater marshes.

8 Lake Apopka Wildlife Drive

2803 Lust Rd, Apopka ■ 386-329-4404 ■ Open sunrise–sunset Fri–Sun ■ www.sjrwmd.com/LANS

This birding and wildlife drive is just an 11-mile (18-km) trip around the north shore of the fourth largest lake in Florida. Visitors can see nearly 200 species of birds, turtles, bobcats, otters, raccoons, alligators, snakes, and coyotes.

9 Wekiwa Springs State Park

MAP A4 ■ 1800 Wekiwa Circle, Apopka ■ 407-884-2008 ■ Open 8am–sunset ■ Adm ■ www.floridastateparks.org/park/wekiwasprings

These springs provide a fertile habitat for such species as white-tail deer, gray foxes, bobcats, raccoons, and black bears. They also provide some of the best places for paddling in a boat in Central Florida. Canoe rentals and picnic and camping areas are also available.

10 Tosohatchee Wildlife Management Area

MAP B3 ■ Christmas, 18 miles (29 km) E of Orlando ■ 407-568-5893 ■ Open 8am–sunset ■ Adm

Swamps dotted with hardwood hammocks (islands covered in shady tropical forest) and a 19-mile (30-km) stretch of the St. Johns River combine to make this one of Central Florida's prettiest, unspoiled parks. Look out for wild orchids and other flora. Hawks, eagles, and fox squirrels can be seen from the trails and alligator, otter and turtles are found in the water.

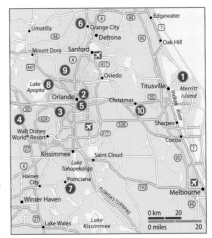

TOP 10 Places to Cool Off

Refreshing slides, pools, and pipes at Aquatica® at SeaWorld®

① Aquatica®

This unique water park (see p104) at SeaWorld® allows you to swim through sealife in a high-speed tube slide. Half-pipes and giant wave pools also keep you entertained. Popular rides include Ihu's Breakaway Falls®, a tower slide that sends riders on a 40-ft (12-m) vertical drop before being swept into a steep waterslide, and Taumata Racer®, a fast contested mat ride.

Blizzard Beach's frosty runs

② Blizzard Beach

Currently claiming the top spot among Orlando's water parks, Blizzard Beach (see p97) has a uniquely themed twist: it's what a ski resort would be like if it started to melt, as waterslides replace ski runs. With seven waterslides and some excellent rides, a wave pool, and kids' areas, it can reach capacity early and close to new admissions until later in the day.

③ Discovery Cove®

Need to unwind on a tropical beach or snorkel over coral reefs? This exclusive (daily entry is limited to 1,000 people) attraction (see p103) offers the features and personalized services of an upscale island resort. Admission is not cheap, but includes everything from lunch to wet suits and sun block. It gets booked up fast so reserve your ticket at least 2 months in advance.

④ Fun2Dive Scuba, Snorkeling, and Manatee Tours

MAP A1 ▪ 2880 Seabreeze Point, Crystal River ▪ 352-228-2279 ▪ Adm ▪ www.fun2dive.com

Whether swimming, snorkeling, or simply watching from the boat, Fun2Dive gives you the opportunity to get closer to manatees than you ever thought possible. Full-day tours run year-round, but the best time to go is migration season from November through March. Groups are kept to six or under, and drinks, snorkeling gear, and sunscreen are provided. Best for ages 5 and up.

5 Orlando's Natural Springs

Orlando may be better known for its not-so-natural attractions, but it does boast some beautiful unspoiled scenery. As well as Wekiwa Springs (see p55) and Blue Spring State Park (see p55), there's DeLeon Springs State Park, Alexander and Juniper Springs, and Silver Springs State Park. All offer a variety of activities, such as snorkeling, paddleboat rentals, fishing, hiking, and kayaking.

6 Lakefront Park

This family-oriented park (see p115) includes a marina, a children's playground, picnic areas with grills, a performing arts pavilion, walking and biking trails, a white sand beach, beach volleyball courts, and a water fountain playground with a great view of picturesque East Lake Tohopekaliga.

7 Typhoon Lagoon

This Disney water park (see p97) is an enthralling mix of slides, tubes, and the largest wave pool in the US. It's suited to families with pre-teen children who'll appreciate the gentler nature of the attractions. One standout is Humunga Kowabanga, where visitors shoot down a near-vertical five-story drop. Wannabe surfers can pay an extra fee for lessons at the wave pool outside of regular opening hours.

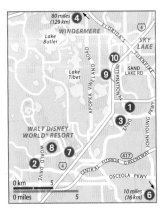

Mount Mayday at Typhoon Lagoon

8 Splash Pads at Disney's Epcot®

MAP G2 ▪ 1200 Epcot Resort Blvd ▪ 407-939-7679 ▪ Adm ▪ www.disneyworld.com

Splash pads are integrated into several attractions throughout Walt Disney World®, but these ones, near Mission Space and Test Track, are there for no other reason than to help hot and tired visitors of all ages cool off. Dancing water fountains and bubbling water provide relief from the heat and humidity.

9 CoCo Key Water Resort

MAP T3 ▪ 407-351-2626 ▪ Open winter: 11am–5pm; summer: 11am–9pm ▪ Adm ▪ www.cocokeyorlando.com

With 14 slides and three heated pools, the outdoor water park here is perfect for splashing around all day. In addition the resort is home to three restaurants and an arcade. Tickets for the water park are sold separately.

10 Universal's Volcano Bay™

MAP E3 ▪ Adventure Way ▪ 407-363-8000 ▪ Open most days 9am–5pm (seasonal times vary) ▪ Adm ▪ www.universalorlando.com

This astonishing volcanic island-themed park will satisfy thrill-seekers with its intense body slides and high-speed rides, but there are plenty of calmer attractions, including winding rivers, sandy beaches, and several play areas. Resort-style facilities are located throughout the park.

Spas

① Mandara Spa at the Loews Portofino Bay Hotel

MAP T1 ▪ 5601 Universal Blvd ▪ 407-503-1244 ▪ Open 8am–8pm daily

A variety of indulgent massages, facials, and body treatments await guests at this Balinese-inspired spa. Guests of the hotel can arrange in-room massages. A sauna, full-service salon, and a fitness center round out the offerings.

② Senses Spa at Disney's Grand Floridian Resort & Spa

MAP F1 ▪ 4401 Floridian Way ▪ 407-824-2332 ▪ Open 8am–8pm daily

The spa at Disney's Victorian-style resort offers a host of pampering services including water and massage therapies, aromatherapy, body wraps, and masks. Special services for kids aged 4–12 are available, if accompanied by an adult.

③ Spa at the Four Seasons Resort Orlando

MAP F2 ▪ 10100 Dream Tree Blvd, Lake Buena Vista ▪ 407-313-7777 ▪ Open 8am–9pm daily ▪ www.fourseasons.com/orlando/spa

A serene oasis where guests can refresh body, mind, and spirit through an array of treatments, from touch therapy to body polishes, and facials. Kids can be transformed into royal princesses and knights with makeup, costumes, and hairstyling.

Spa at the Four Seasons Resort

Relaxing treatment, Mokara Spa

④ Mokara Spa at the Omni Orlando Resort

1500 Masters Blvd, Championsgate ▪ 407-390-6603 ▪ Open 9am–7pm Mon–Sat, 10am–6pm Sun ▪ www.mokaraspas.com/orlando

This beautiful resort has a first-class spa with state-of-the-art treatments and a deluxe fitness facility. From aromatherapy facials to sports massages, clients can take a break from the crowds at this secret resort and have a day of pampering.

⑤ Senses Spa at Disney's Saratoga Springs Resort

MAP G2 ▪ 1960 Broadway, Lake Buena Vista ▪ 407-939-7727 ▪ Open 9am–6pm daily ▪ www.disneyworld.com/spas

The spa at this resort has a range of massage therapies (including hydromassage), body treatments, facials, pedicures, and manicures. Treatments can be selected individually or as part of a full-day package. Reservations must be made by phone in advance.

(6) Relâche Spa at the Gaylord Palms

MAP G3 ▪ 6000 W. Osceola Pkwy, Kissimmee ▪ 407-586-4772 ▪ Open 9am–8pm Mon–Sat, 9am–7pm Sun

This full-service spa offers an array of relaxing treatments including aromatherapy massage, organic facial treatments tailored to your skin's needs, moisturizing manicures, and exfoliating pedicures. Hairstyling and salon services are also offered.

(7) Poseidon Spa at Grand Bohemian

MAP P3 ▪ 325 S. Orange Ave ▪ 407-581-4838 ▪ Open 9am–8pm Mon–Sat, 10am–5pm Sun ▪ www.grandbohemianhotel.com

The Grand Bohemian is a landmark luxury hotel, and the Poseidon Spa only adds to its acclaim. This relaxing spa offers several therapeutic treatments and massages, facials, manicures, and pedicures. In-room services are also available.

(8) Nèu Lotus Spa at the Renaissance Orlando at SeaWorld®

MAP T5 ▪ 6677 Sea Harbor Dr ▪ 407-248-7428 ▪ Open 9am–7pm

There's a full line of traditional spa services here, including massages (Swedish, deep tissue, and reflexology); body treatments (polishes and wraps); and a selection of facials, one of which is designed to introduce teenagers to the basics of skin care. In-room massages are available to resort guests for an additional charge.

Seating area, the Waldorf Astoria Spa

(9) The Waldorf Astoria Spa

MAP G2 ▪ 14200 Bonnet Creek Resort Ln ▪ 407-597-5360 ▪ Open 9am–9pm daily ▪ www.waldorfastoriaorlando.com

Relax in the luxuriously calm, serene atmosphere at the Waldorf Astoria, and enjoy a range of pampering treatments, including body therapies, massages, and facials, as well as a selection of salon services. There's also a steam room and Jacuzzi on site, plus a tea lounge.

(10) The Spa at the Ritz-Carlton Grande Lakes

MAP F4 ▪ 4012 Central Florida Pkwy ▪ 407-393-4200 ▪ Open 9am–7pm daily ▪ www.ritzcarlton.com/en/Properties/Orlando/Spa

A day in this spa is time well spent. Start with a facial in one of the spa's 40 treatment rooms. Go for a swim in the private 4,000-sq-ft (375-sq-m) outdoor lap pool, or enjoy a relaxing massage followed by a visit to the boutique. End your outing with dinner at Norman's.

TOP 10 Sports and Outdoor Activities

ESPN Wide World of Sports Complex

1 ESPN Wide World of Sports Complex

MAP G2 ▪ Walt Disney World®
▪ 407-828-3267 ▪ Hours vary ▪ Adm
▪ www.espnwwos.com

Watch events or participate in 60 sports at this vast facility, with 10 world-class fields, courts, and arenas. ESPN Wide World of Sports merchandise is also available here.

2 Tennis

Disney: 407-939-7529; courts open 9am–10pm daily; adm ▪ Grand Cypress: MAP F2; 1 N. Jacaranda; 407-621-1991; open 8am–5pm daily; adm

There are some great clay courts at Disney's Grand Floridian Resort & Spa, Saratoga Springs Resort & Spa, Disney's Bay Lake Tower, BoardWalk Inn & Villas, Old Key West, and The Swan & Dolphin. Beyond Disney, the nearby Grand Cypress Racquet Club has twelve excellent courts.

3 Horseback Riding

Tri-Circle-D Ranch, Disney's Fort Wilderness Resort: MAP F2; 407-939-7529; open 8:30am–4pm daily; adm

Tri-Circle-D Ranch at Disney's Fort Wilderness Resort offers 45-minute guided trail rides on horseback or in a carriage through the woodlands. Smaller children can take a pony ride.

4 Cycling

Bike Barn, Disney's Fort Wilderness Resort: MAP F2; 407-824-2900; open 9am–5pm daily; adm

Get away on Disney's scenic bike trails. You can rent single- and multi-speed bikes for kids and adults at the Fort Wilderness Resort's Bike Barn. Tandems and cycles with baby seats and training wheels are also available. Two-, four-, and six-person Surrey bicycles are available for rent at a number of Disney locations.

5 Boating

Walt Disney World® lakes: MAP F1–G2; open at least 9am–5pm daily; adm

Many of the artificial lakes around Walt Disney World® have small motor-boats and pontoon boats for rent. There are also paddleboats for those who prefer more of a workout.

6 Swimming

Swimmers are spoiled for choice with a mild temperature year round, two sea coasts, springs and lakes. Hotel pools (see pp142–7) range from lazy rivers to quiet spa pools.

Swimming at Disney's BoardWalk Resort

7 Watersports

Paddleboard Orlando:
MAP C5; hours vary; hourly rentals;
www.paddleboardorlando.com

Winter Park has a number of lakes, which are perfect for paddle boarding. Paddleboard Orlando at Lake Killarney offer classes by qualified instructors.

8 Surfing

Typhoon Lagoon: MAP G2; 407-939-7529; classes at 6:45–9:30am & 5:30–8:30pm; book in advance; adm
■ **Ron Jon Surf School: MAP B3;** 321-868-1980; call for details; adm

According to the state's surf addicts, Disney's Typhoon Lagoon *(see p57)* has wave-making down to a fine art. Ron Jon Surf School on Cocoa Beach holds regular classes for beginners.

Fishing expedition in Central Florida

9 Fishing

Pro Bass Guide Service: 407-877-9676; open daily; adm

Land your dinner with Pro Bass Guide Service, a Winter Garden outfit that specializes in guided bass-fishing trips to some of Central Florida's most picturesque rivers and lakes. There are also offshore expeditions for saltwater species.

10 Wagon rides

Disney's Fort Wilderness Resort: MAP F2; 407-824-2900; rides are available evenings daily; adm

Take an old-fashioned wagon ride along the scenic trails at Fort Wilderness. Expect plenty of singing and dancing, and a good-time atmosphere on this 25-minute ride.

TOP 10 SPORTING EVENTS

Stadium view, Florida Citrus Bowl

1 Florida Citrus Bowl
407-849-2020 ■ Jan 1
Annual college football showdown between the no. 2 teams.

2 Walt Disney World® Marathon
407-824-4321 ■ Early Jan ■ www.disneyworld.com
Annual 26-mile (42-km) race with entrants from around the world.

3 Bike Weeks
866-761-7223 ■ Early Feb
Two weeks of motor action at Daytona Beach, ending with the Daytona 500.

4 Orlando City Soccer
407-478-4007 ■ Feb–Aug
Watch professional teams in action.

5 Arnold Palmer Invitational
407-876-2888 ■ Mar
A top golf tournament played in memory of golf legend Arnold Palmer.

6 Atlanta Braves Spring Training
407-939-7712 ■ Mar ■ www.braves.com
Catch baseball team Atlanta Braves in pre-season training.

7 Orlando Pride
855-675-2489 ■ Apr–Oct
Watch Orlando's National Women's Soccer League team.

8 Silver Spurs Rodeo
407-677-6336 ■ Jun & Oct ■ www.silverspursrodeo.com
These large-scale rodeo events are held twice a year in Kissimmee.

9 Children's Miracle Network Classic
407-939-4653 ■ Mid-Oct
Tour pros in a week of golfing events.

10 Orlando Magic
407-440-7000 ■ Oct–Apr
Don't miss the NBA team in season.

TOP10 Golf Courses

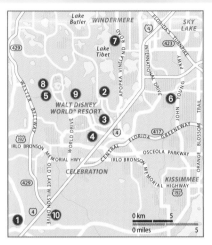

2 Villas of Grand Cypress Golf Club

MAP F2 ▪ 1 N. Jacaranda ▪ 407-239-4700 ▪ www.grandcypress.com

Jack Nicklaus designed these highly rated 45 holes. The New Course was inspired by the Old Course at St Andrews in Scotland. The club is semi-private with some public tee times. (Max yd: 6,906 [6,315 m]. USGA rating: 74.4.)

3 Disney's Lake Buena Vista

MAP F2 ▪ Buena Vista Dr ▪ 407-938-4653 ▪ www.disneyworld.com

This tight course has heavily bunkered fairways, a dense pine forest, and an unusual island green on the 7th hole. (Max yd: 6,819 [6,325 m]. USGA rating: 72.7.)

1 ChampionsGate

MAP H1 ▪ 1400 Masters Blvd ▪ 407-787-4653 ▪ Lessons available ▪ www.championsgategolf.com

Greg Norman created two 18-hole courses (the National and the International) for this vast family-friendly resort community southwest of Disney, featuring woods, wetlands, and open land, in addition to plenty of activities for those who choose not to golf. Between them they have 13 water holes, and share double greens at the 4th and 16th holes. (Max yd: 7,048 [6,445 m] and 7,407 [6,773 m], respectively. USGA rating: 75.1 & 76.3.)

4 Waldorf Astoria Golf Club

MAP G2 ▪ 14200 Bonnet Creek Resort Ln ▪ 407-597-5500 ▪ www.waldorfastoriaorlando.com

Rees Jones designed this 18-hole course around the contours of a wetland preserve. Impressive pine and cypress stands line the fairways; a 5-tee system accommodates all skill levels. (Max yd: 7,108 [6,500 m]. USGA rating: 74.6.)

Waldorf Astoria Golf Club

Aerial view of Disney's Palm course

5 Disney's Palm
MAP F1 ■ Palm Dr ■ 407-939-4653 ■ Lessons available ■ www.disneyworld.com

This jewel of a course is surrounded by woodlands. Half of its holes have water, and its 94 bunkers create headaches for those whose shots stray. The 18th hole is one of the toughest on the PGA Tour. (Max yd: 6,957 [6,391 m]. USGA rating: 73.)

6 Ritz-Carlton Golf Club Grande Lakes
MAP F4 ■ 4040 Central Florida Pkwy ■ 407-393-4900 ■ Lessons available ■ www.grandelakes.com

This 18-hole Greg Norman course is certified as an Audubon Cooperative Sanctuary. You can enjoy thriving ponds, wetlands, oak, and cypress, while playing on a challenging PGA course. (Max yd: 7,122 [6,512 m]. USGA rating: 73.9)

7 Bay Hill Golf Club & Lodge
MAP E2 ■ 9000 Bay Hill Rd ■ 407-876-2429 ■ www.bayhill.com

Arnold Palmer designed this sweeping out-of-the-way course, located along the Butler chain of lakes. Among the oldest courses in the area, it has been redesigned to include two championship courses, a nine-hole challenge course, and the Arnold Palmer Golf Academy. (Max yd: 7,381 [6,749 m]. USGA rating: none.)

8 Disney's Magnolia
MAP F1 ■ Palm Dr ■ 407-938-4653 ■ Lessons available ■ www.disneyworld.com

Here's a course with forgivingly wide fairways that let you hammer the ball. But don't get reckless: 11 of the 18 holes contain water and the course has 97 bunkers, with many waiting to gobble your miss hits. Part of the PGA's Funai Golf Classic is played here. (Max yd: 7,190 [6,574 m]. USGA rating: 73.9.)

9 Disney's Osprey Ridge
MAP F2 ■ Golf View Dr ■ 407-938-4653 ■ www.disneyworld.com

Arguably the most challenging of Disney's five 18-hole courses, the Tom Fazio-designed Osprey Ridge features native woodlands, elevated tees, fairly large greens, nine water holes, and more than 70 bunkers. *Golf Digest*'s "Places to Play" ranks it among Florida's best public and resort courses. (Max yd: 7,101 [6,493 m]. USGA rating: 74.4.)

Players at Disney's Osprey Ridge

10 Reunion Golf
7599 Gathering Dr ■ 407-396-3196 ■ Lessons available ■ www.reunionresort.com

Nowhere else will you find three signature courses designed by the likes of Jack Nicklaus, Tom Watson, and Arnold Palmer, all in a single location. Each course offers a unique experience – and a unique challenge – whether in the form of rolling hills, smooth long fairways, or strategically placed bunkers. (Max yd: 7,244 [6,624m], USGA rating: Palmer 73.4, Watson 74.7, Nicklaus 76.7.)

🔟 Off the Beaten Path

Forever Florida zip line

1 Forever Florida

Get on horseback, ride a wild coach (a gigantic safari-style vehicle) or go zip-lining at this eco-based attraction (see p114). You may spot alligators, black bear, white-tail deer, hundreds of species of birds, and an array of flora, as you traverse the nine different ecosystems here.

2 Crystal River and Homosassa Springs

MAP A1 ■ River Ventures, 498 S.E. Kings Bay Dr, Crystal River ■ 352-564-8687 ■ Adm ■ www.river ventures.com

A variety of boats tour year-round on the Crystal River and Homosassa Springs, allowing visitors to swim with manatees. Sightings of these gentle creatures are most frequent from late October to late March.

3 The Citrus Tower

MAP A2 ■ 141 N. Hwy 27, Clermont ■ 352-394-4061 ■ Open 9am–5pm Mon–Sat ■ Adm ■ www. citrustower.com

Built in 1956 on one of Florida's highest points, this venerable 226-ft-(69-m-) tall observation tower gives a 360-degree view of the rolling hills and hundreds of spring-fed lakes in the eight counties surrounding it. The tip of its highest antenna reaches a height of 500 ft (152 m) above sea level.

4 Florida Southern College

MAP B2 ■ 111 Lake Hollingsworth Dr, Lakeland ■ 863-680-4597 ■ Visitor center: open 9:30am–4pm daily

In the late 1930s, architect Frank Lloyd Wright designed 12 campus buildings at this college – the largest collection of his buildings on one site. Highlights include the Annie Pfeiffer Chapel, the Roux Library, the Danforth Chapel, and the Esplanades. Pick up a walking-tour map from the visitor center.

5 Lakeridge Winery

MAP A2 ■ 19239 US-27, Clermont ■ 800-768-9463 ■ Open 9am–5pm Mon–Sat; tours every 30 mins

Winery tours begin with a 15-minute video on the wine-making process in Florida, then you'll get to visit the production area and see the vineyards. Finally, you can taste a selection of Lakeridge's award-winning wines. The winery also holds various festivals and music events through-out the year.

Following pages Performance at Orlando Shakes

6 Central Florida Zoo and Botanical Gardens

MAP A2 ▪ 3755 NW. Hwy 17-92, Sanford ▪ Visitors Center: open 9am–5pm daily; 407-323-4450; adm; www.centralfloridazoo.org

Beneath the zoo's dense canopy of foliage, visitors can observe the residents (from howler monkeys to bald eagles) at close quarters. Some areas are more exciting than others but, on the whole, this makes for a rewarding trip.

7 Eco Tours at the Ritz Carlton and JW Marriott Grande Lakes

MAP F4 ▪ 4012 Central Florida Pkwy ▪ 407-206-2400 ▪ Tours 9:30am & 1pm daily

A two-hour guided canoe or kayak tour of Shingle Creek, the head-waters to the Florida Everglades, gives guests a taste of old Florida. While paddling, you'll learn the history of Shingle Creek from your water guides. Be sure to keep an eye out for alligators, bald eagles, osprey, and barred owls.

8 Boggy Creek Airboat Rides

This ride (see p116), appropriate for everyone in the family, offers a unique chance to see nature from aboard an airboat. Speeding (and sometimes stopping) through the wetlands and marshes of the headwaters of the Florida Everglades, you'll see turtles, alligators, birds, and more. The best time to see the wildlife is early in the morning (on a hot day) or in the evening (on a cooler day).

Interior of Stetson Mansion

9 Stetson Estate

MAP A2 ▪ 1031 Camphor La, Deland ▪ www.stetsonmansion.com ▪ Adm; no credit cards

Take a tour of Florida's most opulent and historic home and estate. Built for hatmaker and philanthropist John B. Stetson, the house has been restored to showcase its unusual blend of cottage, Gothic, Tudor, Moorish, and Polynesian styles.

10 St. Johns Rivership Company

MAP A2 ▪ 433 N. Palmetto Ave ▪ 321-441-3030 ▪ Adm ▪ www.stjohnsrivershipco.com

Operating out of historic Sanford, the 1946-built triple-decked Barbara-Lee offers daily cruises along the scenic St Johns River. It's a truly civilized way to catch a glimpse of the Florida that tourists rarely see.

Boggy Creek Airboat Rides

🔟 Live Music Venues

Downtown gig at The Social

1 The Social

This intimate Downtown club *(see p122)* serves up an eclectic mix of live music from established acts and up-and-coming artists. Sounds range from alternative rock to funk, jazz, and dance, with local DJs also gracing the club's legendary stage. For years, the club's policy of booking top national touring acts meant it was the shining light of Orlando's live music scene. Now competition from larger clubs is stiffer, but this tiny spot, with its stylishly raw decor, remains O-Town's favorite venue to enjoy live music.

2 House of Blues®

Wall-to-wall original folk art gives this giant venue *(see p99)* a funky look. But like all things in the Disney empire, the decor hides a modern, smooth-running machine. HOB books amazing acts in every genre, from hip-hop to death metal. Shows here start and end on time, and the sound system is crystal clear. The one flaw is a lack of any seating with a stage view, so be prepared to be on your feet all night.

3 Blue Martini

MAP T3 ▪ 9101 International Dr ▪ 407-447-2583

Serving up 42 signature martinis and specialty cocktails of every flavor and color, this vibrant spot – with live music nightly – is popular with young professionals, in part thanks to a post-work happy hour for sharing plates. Tapas and a light menu are on offer too. The outdoor patio bar is a good place to mingle.

4 Bösendorfer Lounge

The lounge music craze that once swept the nation is now only for serious practitioners. This elegant hotel bar *(see p122)* is the perfect place to sip cocktails and admire the performers in evening dress, who sing near the $250,000 Bösendorfer Grand piano.

5 The Plaza Live

MAP D5 ▪ 425 N. Bumby Ave ▪ 407-228-1220 ▪ www.plazalive orlando.com

Originally the city's first two-screen movie house, this is the city's premier live concert venue, hosting bands, comedians, and cultural events. There's a seated balcony and lots of standing space.

The Colosseum-style Hard Rock Live at night

6 Hard Rock Live
MAP T1 ■ 6050 Universal Boulevard, CityWalk™ ■ 407-351-5483 ■ www.hardrock.com/live/locations/orlando/

Hard Rock offers a comfortable setting for concerts, with balcony seating and good stage views. The grand ballroom decor is more appropriate for acts that want to perform in an elegant setting, so it's not that surprising that top R&B artists such as Maxwell and Erykah Badu play here.

7 Tin Roof
MAP T3 ■ 8371 International Dr ■ 407-270-7926

Making a great addition to the lively ICON Orlando 360™ (home of the ICON Orlando™; see p106), the Tin Roof has a vintage 1950s vibe, and serves up lunch and dinner along with nightly live entertainment. Performances come from both famous and not-so-famous acts, ensuring that the entertainment here is an ever-changing affair.

8 Bongos Cuban Cafe®
MAP G2 ■ Disney Springs™ ■ 407-828-0999

This lively venue combines Old Havana and Miami. As well as delicious Cuban food, Bongos serves up furious salsa rhythms. There is dancing every night, and great live music Fridays and Saturdays.

9 Howl at the Moon
Dance till you drop at this lively I-Drive location that's part bar, part concert venue (see p108). Bands belt out favorites from the 1980s and 1990s, along with today's top party hits. The drinks menu is extensive, including a slew of signature cocktails.

Logo for Howl at the Moon

10 Atlantic Dance Hall & Jellyrolls
MAP W2 ■ Disney's BoardWalk ■ Adm ■ Atlantic Dance Hall: 407-939-5277; Closed Sun & Mon ■ Jellyrolls: 407-560-8770

Travel back in time to dance at the glamorous dance halls of the 1930s and 40s. Atlantic Dance Hall (see p142) features wonderful Art Deco interiors and is ideally located for those staying at a Disney resort. Next door at Jellyrolls (see p72), pianos duel nightly, playing guests' shouted requests. Both venues are for ages 21 and up.

Exterior of Atlantic Dance Hall

📥🔟 Clubs

by 70 tons of hand-carved ice, guests can sip on chilled cocktails served in ice glasses, while wearing the cozy coats and mittens provided. Time is limited, but afterward you can warm up at the Fire Lounge, dancing and drinking all night long.

③ Tier
MAP P3 ■ 20 E. Central Blvd ■ 407-222-9732 ■ Adm ■ www.tier nightclub.com

Over 10,000 sq ft (3,048 sq m) of space to dance the night away, with resident and guest DJs spinning tunes Tuesday through Sunday. There are VIP tables, private skyboxes, and five bars.

① EVE
MAP P3 ■ 110 S. Orange Ave ■ 407-602-7462 ■ Adm ■ Closed Mon & Tue ■ www.eveorlando.com

The place to see and be seen, EVE is a luxury club, rivaling the nightlife venues of LA, Vegas, or Miami. Inside are three distinct spaces: the V lounge, Chandelier Room nightclub, and balcony Garden Terrace. State-of-the-art sound, lighting, and sparkling crystal chandeliers make for an unparalleled experience.

② ICEBAR
Chill out at the coolest club in town, where temperatures reach well below freezing (see p108). Surrounded

④ Vyce Lounge
MAP P3 ■ 112 S. Orange Ave ■ www.vycelounge.com

Orlando's only boutique nightclub – meaning you won't have to share the space with thousands of others – boasts floor-to-ceiling engraved Venetian mirrors and an LED ceiling. Expect a different theme every night.

⑤ Monkey Bar
MAP P3 ■ 26 Wall St ■ 407-849-0471 ■ Closed Sun, Mon ■ Adm

Walk through the downstairs Tiki Bar and ride the elevator up to this trendy Wall Street hideaway. There's food as well as quirky drinks and live music. Enjoy half-price martinis during happy hour (4–7pm Tue–Fri).

Ice sculptures at ICEBAR

Performers at The Beacham

6 The Beacham

The Beacham *(see p122)* is housed in a Downtown Orlando theater building that once hosted the famous Vaudeville acts of the 1920s. It went on to become the city's main movie theater before being turned into a nightclub, initially promoted by Paris Hilton. It is a 1,250-seat live music venue and a buzzing nightclub, with high-tech sound and light systems and a large dance floor. National touring acts appear regularly; on other evenings, DJs set the pace. Friday night is Ladies' Night. A strict dress code is enforced.

7 Mango's Tropical Cafe

Come to this vast entertainment complex *(see p73)* for dinner and a show, or to dance the night away. Seating for the first dinner show begins at 6:30pm, with a second, more risqué show at 10pm (without dinner, although there's a short late-night menu). Dancers, most rather scantily clad, perform the samba and conga, with a variety of acts taking to the stage. Salsa classes are also available at select times.

8 the groove™

The theme changes every night at this Universal CityWalk™ dance club *(see p108)*, with music from the 1970s and 1980s, current dance hits, Latin, techno, and more. The club area has a giant psychedelic dance floor, but the smaller areas – the Candle Room, Blue Room, and Red Room – are great for more intimate partying. the groove™ is an attractive alternative for teens, too, with dedicated teen nights on Mondays and Wednesdays.

9 Bar 17 Bistro

MAP E3 ▪ 6725 Adventure Way ▪ 407-503-6000

The 17th floor of the Aventura Hotel is home to this lounge and small-plates eatery, the first rooftop bar and grill from Universal. It has floor-to-ceiling glass windows and affords fabulous views of Hogwarts™ Castle and the theme parks. Custom cocktails and urban international flavors find pride of place on the menu of this hip, comfortable space. It is close to Universal's theme parks and other hotels in the area.

High-energy dancing at The Attic

10 The Attic

MAP P3 ▪ 68 E. Pine St ▪ 407-403-1161 ▪ Adm ▪ www.theatticorlando.com

The Attic is an upstairs venue with an atmosphere recalling a hip city loft space with exposed brick. It is Orlando's premier EDM (electronic dance music) venue, so expect a high-energy atmosphere, with plenty of lasers. Tuesday through Saturday local DJs spin the hottest tracks all night long. There's a smart-casual dress code, which means no shorts or sandals for guys.

TOP10 Gay and Lesbian Nightlife

Visitors swarming the Parliament House Resort club

1 Parliament House Resort
MAP P2 ■ 410 N. Orange Blossom Trail ■ 407-425-7571

The internationally known Parliament House is one of the southeast's premier gay resorts, boasting non-stop entertainment. In addition to a 130-room hotel, there's a pulsating dance club, a piano bar, a country and western bar, a video bar, lakeside beach parties, and more.

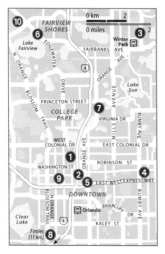

2 Hamburger Mary's
MAP D4 ■ 110 W. Church St ■ 321-319-0600 ■ www.hamburger marys.com/orlando

Tasty appetizers, juicy burgers, and delicious desserts are on the menu, but it's the evening entertainment you'll want to stick around for. Think dining with divas, and you'll soon get the picture. Shows, ranging from an interactive drag show and cabaret to a night of trivia, start at 7 or 7:30pm, with a Broadway Brunch on Sundays.

3 Park Social
This trendy cocktail den (see p128) in Winter Park has the DJ spinning vinyl favorites with a retro feel. Sit back and relax on wingback chairs and vintage couches, set amid an ambience that harks back to the '70s and '80s. It draws an extremely trendy crowd.

4 Southern Nights
MAP P3 ■ 375 S. Bumby Ave ■ 407-412-5039

Southern Nights is a mega-club with several bars and performance spaces to choose from. It hosts regular theme nights and fancy-dress evenings, and is famed for its elaborate female impersonation shows and lively diva-hosted dance parties. There's also an outdoor patio for unwinding and relaxing, and a game room with pool tables, darts, and video games. Happy hour is 4pm–9pm every Wednesday.

Bösendorfer Lounge

Signature cocktails mixed with the soulful sound of jazz draw an upscale crowd to this stylish hotel haunt *(see p122)*. Maybe it's the heavy drapes, the dark wood, or the well-tuned ennui of some patrons, but you feel wealthy just being here. It's very popular with cabaret fans on Friday and Saturday nights, when you'll be treated to live performances – whether it's the tinkling of Imperial Grand Bösendorfer piano keys or hits sung by jazz and soul groups.

6 BarCodes
MAP L1 ■ 4453 Edgewater Dr ■ 407-412-6917

Located north of the city, this fun night-spot attracts a more mature clientele than the 20-something crowds else-where. As it's just down the road from Hank's, don't be surprised to see patrons bouncing between both bars on any given evening. There's leather night the last Saturday of every month, karaoke on Mondays, and underwear parties Wednesday and Sunday.

7 Savoy Orlando
MAP P3 ■ 1913 N. Orange Ave ■ 407-270-4685

A sophisticated North Orange lounge that caters for an upscale crowd of mostly professional gay men. High

Bar display at Savoy Orlando

bar tables, black leather stools, and crystal chandeliers give the club a classy air.

8 Mango's Tropical Cafe
MAP T3 ■ 8126 International Dr ■ 407-673-4422

Enjoy the 55,000 sq ft (5,110 sq m) of high-energy glamor, lights, live music, and dancing at Mango's *(see p108)*. The Latin Connection Band plays for the dancers on the main stage. However, the main attraction is the dinner and show that features Michael Jackson and Celia Cruz impersonations. Visitors can take salsa lessons and join the nightly Conga Line.

Vibrant interior of Mango's Tropical Cafe

9 Stonewall
MAP P3 ■ 741 W. Church St ■ 407-373-0888

Everything from leather-clad dancers to underwear nights makes this a go-to for the local gay community. There are daily happy hours, bingo and poker nights, and karaoke on Friday nights.

10 Hank's
MAP L1 ■ 5026 Edgewater Dr ■ 407-291-2399

Hank's has been open for over 20 years and is one of Orlando's oldest gay bars. Pool tables, darts, video games, and a jukebox make this unpretentious beer and wine bar a casual hangout. The Back Room, the adjoining adult store, is open nightly.

Dinner Shows

1 Hoop-Dee-Doo Musical Revue

Reserve well in advance for this show (see p99), Disney's most popular "chow-and-cheer" night, at the Fort Wilderness Resort. The jokes are silly, the stars dress in costumes from Broadway's *Oklahoma!*, and if you don't join in the singalong fun, the actors and audience will keep on at you until you do. Dinner is all-you-can-eat fried chicken and barbecue ribs. There's also a vegetarian menu, available with 24 hours' notice.

2 Sleuths Mystery Dinner Shows

MAP T1 ■ 8267 International Dr ■ 407-363-1985 ■ Show times vary

Twelve different shows are staged in three theaters over the course of a month, each with a suspicious death, and a twist before the mystery is finally uncovered. The dinner includes hors d'oeuvres before the show, then your choice of honey-glazed Cornish game hen, prime rib, or lasagna (with or without meat), plus side dishes, dessert, and unlimited beer, wine, and sodas. In addition to the regular dinner show, Sleuths also offers select after-hours productions – mainly comedy shows – aimed at an adult audience.

Dinner show at Medieval Times

3 Medieval Times

MAP H3 ■ 4510 W. Vine St, Kissimmee ■ 407-396-2900 ■ Pre-arrange vegetarian entrées ■ Show times vary

Horses take a secondary role at this spectacle. Instead, the action heroes are knights who fence, joust, and otherwise raise the roof while you feast on barbecued ribs and roasted chicken with your fingers (after all, this is the 11th century). If you arrive early, you get the chance to tour a re-created medieval village.

4 Pirate's Dinner Adventure

MAP T2 ■ 6400 Carrier Dr ■ 407-206-5100 ■ 6 & 8:30pm daily

The swashbuckling actors entertain with comedy, drama, and music on a 46 ft- (14m-) long replica of a Spanish galleon in an indoor "lagoon." The dinner buffet features beef, chicken, or vegetarian pasta, with free soft drinks and beer during the show. Afterward, there's a Buccaneer Bash Dance Party.

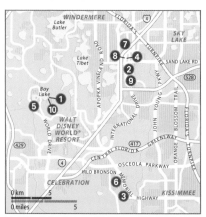

5 Disney's Spirit of Aloha Dinner Show

MAP F1 ▪ Disney's Polynesian Village Resort ▪ 407-824-2000 ▪ 5:15 & 8:15pm daily

High-energy performers from Hawaii, New Zealand, and Tahiti show off their hula, ceremonial, and fire dancing in an open-air theater. Meanwhile, tuck into the all-you-can-eat dinner, with roast pork and chicken, fried rice, vegetables, and fruit. Learn to make *leis* and do the hula in the pre-show.

6 Capone's Dinner & Show

MAP G3 ▪ 4740 W. Irlo Bronson Memorial Hwy ▪ 407-397-2378 ▪ Mid-Jun–mid-Aug: 8pm; mid-Aug–mid-Jun: 7:30pm

Head back to the 1930s to visit Al Capone's notorious speakeasy, a place where pseudo-mobsters and their molls entertain guests with a lot of song and dance. The all-you-can-eat buffet includes pasta, sausage, baked chicken, ham, and vegetables, plus any beer, wine, coffee, iced tea, and sodas you care to drink.

7 Wantilan Luau Dinner Show

MAP E3 ▪ 6300 Hollywood Way ▪ 407-503-3463 ▪ 6pm Sat

Set in a tropical paradise at Universal's Royal Pacific Resort, this Polynesian luau serves up an ample all-you-can-eat buffet of pit-roasted pig, marinated beef, and the catch of the day, along with tropical fruits, desserts,

Learning the hula at Wantilan Luau

and more. While dining, you'll be entertained by traditional hula and fire dancers.

8 Titanic Gala Dinner Event

MAP E3 ▪ 7324 International Dr ▪ 407-248-1166 ▪ Pre-arrange vegetarian entrées ▪ 7pm Fri & Sat

Experience first-class dining aboard the *Titanic*, as participants re-enact the retirement dinner of Captain E.J. Smith on the fateful night when it sank. Includes a tour of the "ship".

The Outta Control improv-style show

9 The Outta Control Magic Comedy Dinner Show

MAP T4 ▪ WonderWorks, 9067 International Dr ▪ 407-351-8800 ▪ 6pm & 8pm daily

The audience becomes a part of the show in Tony Brent's 90-minute interactive mixture of magic and fast-paced improvisational comedy. Impersonations and mind-reading are accompanied by delicious all-you-can-eat pizza, popcorn, beer, and soda. For all ages.

10 Mickey's Backyard BBQ

MAP G2 ▪ 4510 Fort Wilderness Trail, Lake Buena Vista ▪ 407-939-3463 ▪ 5:15pm in season

Enjoy a foot-stompin' good time at this all-you-can-eat BBQ, with the Fort Wilderness Campground as backdrop. The hearty hoedown menu includes ribs, hot dogs, corn on the cob, and all the trimmings. Mickey and friends join in with the line dancing.

TOP 10 High-End Restaurants

The interior of the Waldorf Astoria's Bull & Bear Steakhouse

1 Bull & Bear Steakhouse

Modeled after the original in New York City, this sophisticated restaurant (see p100) in the Waldorf Astoria oozes style and elegance. The menu focuses on prime meats and seafood, often prepared tableside. Boutique vintners are on the wine list.

2 Victoria & Albert's

The prices tend to limit this place (see p100) to special occasions, but trust the first-class food, fine wine, and faultless staff to make a memorable visit. It's decorated like Queen Victoria's dining room, and each table gets its very own pair of servers. Take advantage of the wine-pairings (a glass with each of the five courses); it's cheaper and more varied than buying a bottle.

3 VIVO Italian Kitchen™

A sleek, modern setting and heirloom family recipes await diners at this Italian restaurant (see p100). The open-view kitchen allows a glimpse of piping-hot pizzas sliding out of the oven, along with fresh pasta, sauces and assorted meat, vegetarian and seafood dishes being prepared by the chefs. Each meal is a savory delight, created with the finest ingredients available.

4 Christner's Prime Steak & Lobster

An Orlando staple for over 25 years, Christner's (see p129) serves superb cuts of beef and prime seafood, and decadent desserts, along with a choice of over 4,500 bottles of wine from Cabernets to Reislings. There's also an elegant piano lounge, and an illusionist performs on some Saturday evenings.

5 Morimoto Asia

A spectacular Disney flagship restaurant (see p100), where exhibition kitchens allow diners the chance to see what happens behind the scenes. Its two floors contain a huge open dining room and intimate dining spaces, as well as an attached sushi bar. The Chinese, Japanese, and Korean dishes range from classics to innovative creations.

Asian delicacies at Morimoto Asia

6 California Grill

The 15th-floor vista gets top marks from both critics and diners in this popular restaurant (see p100). Favorites include seared grouper in a noodle bowl with ginger-crab salad, and you can count on sampling some of the most inventive sushi in town. Unusually, California Gill offers an interesting menu for those who prefer vegetarian. You could also indulge in the leisurely Sunday brunch, taking in the views of Magic Kingdom park while sipping on complimentary mimosas. It's hard to get a table on weekends, though – try to reserve well in advance.

7 Norman's

An elegant restaurant (see p109) located in the Ritz-Carlton, Norman's specializes in a fusion of Latin, European, and Floridian cuisine. World-renowned chef Norman Van Aken holds court when in town, but the kitchen turns out his delicious New World-style menu regardless. Some of the highlights here include a Brazilian conch chowder and barbecued veal chops, and the dining room has lovely views over the gardens and golf course.

8 THE BOATHOUSE

The Landing at Disney Springs™ lays claim to some of the newest and most innovative restaurants in the area, among them THE BOATHOUSE (see p100), with its fantastic waterfront views. The menu focuses on premium steaks and chops, along with a selection of Florida's freshest seafood. After dinner, you can take a leisurely tour of the lake aboard a vintage boat, the Captain's Italian water taxi, or one of the unique Amphicars. Champagne and wine-tasting cruises are also available.

9 Todd English's bluezoo

Celebrate the ocean in a dining room that feels like an underwater scene. Awarded for its food, wine list and interior design, this restaurant (see p100) also has a lounge with a separate menu for the bar. Asian, Tuscan, and American touches influence the superb fish menu. Meat dishes are also available.

Elegant dining room at The Boheme

10 The Boheme

The signature restaurant (see p123) of the Westin Grand Bohemian Hotel is a key business venue as well as a top romantic destination, serving classic dishes with a modern twist. Menu highlights range from Southern crab cakes to filet mignon and rack of lamb. Sip a martini before dinner in the hip Bösendorfer Lounge.

TOP 10 Family Restaurants

Eye-popping decor at T-REX™

① T-REX™

A paradise for pint-sized paleontologists, this restaurant *(see p100)* boasts dense prehistoric plant life everywhere you turn, along with bubbling geysers, meteor showers, and an endless number of prehistoric special effects (including very life-like animatronic dinosaurs).

② Baja Burrito Kitchen

The draw here *(see p123)* is the fresh and tasty Californian and Mexican cuisine, such as tacos, quesadillas, fajitas, and burritos, stuffed with lean meat and sour cream and cheese.

③ Sci-Fi Dine-in Theater Restaurant

Step back in time and into your car at this popular restau-rant *(see p101)* featuring a very convincing drive-in movie theme, complete with B-movies playing on the big screen under a starlit sky. Food is secondary to the atmosphere, but the sandwiches and burgers will surely fill you up. Advance reservations are advised.

④ Coral Reef Restaurant

A 600,000-gallon (272,600-liter) floor-to-ceiling aquarium is the calming backdrop to this restaurant *(see p101)*. Despite the mainly fish and seafood menu, it's very child-friendly. Try the sautéed rock shrimp in lemon cream sauce.

⑤ Whispering Canyon Cafe

This Western-themed restaurant *(see p100)* encourages horsing around, with spirited singalongs and hobbyhorse races round the restaurant all acceptable meal-time behavior.

⑥ 50's Prime Time Café

Home-cooked-style comfort foods, from pot roast to meatloaf, are all on the menu here *(see p101)* – and portions are generous. Vintage TV sets showing reruns of *I Love Lucy* add to the 1950s vibe in one of the park's most popular dining spots. If you want a table, you'll need to reserve in advance.

Sign for 50's Prime Time Café

7 Boma – Flavors of Africa

This all-you-can-eat, African-themed restaurant (see p100) is in Disney's Animal Kingdom Lodge. Dishes from more than 50 African countries are served from the open kitchen for breakfast and dinner. There's a good selection of grilled meats, salads, and pastries. The dinner buffet also offers family-friendly options.

8 Café Tu Tu Tango

The menu here (see p109) is described as Spanish tapas but the food is international in flavor, with such diverse nibbles as baked goat's cheese, tuna sashimi, alligator bites, and snapper fingers. Performers (from sword eaters to artists at work) provide the entertainment.

Café Tu Tu Tango artists at work

9 Via Napoli Ristorante e Pizzeria

The southern Italian menu here (see p101) includes delicious thin-crust Neapolitan pizzas that have been cooked in huge wood-fired ovens. Each oven is decorated with a face meant to represent one of Italy's three volcanos.

10 'Ohana

Flavorful meals of skewers (oak-grilled chicken, marinated steak, Asian barbecue pork, and spicy shrimp), stir-fried vegetables, pineapple coconut bread, and more are prepared here (see p100) over an 18-ft (5.5-m) fire pit. Storytelling, shell races, and hula dancing are all part of the fun.

TOP 10 DINE-OUTS WITH DISNEY AND UNIVERSAL CHARACTERS

Cinderella hosts her Royal Table

1 Cinderella's Royal Table
A whole host of Disney characters join you for this one of a kind dining experience in the Cinderella Castle (see p101) at the Magic Kingdom®.

2 Akershus Royal Banquet Hall
Dine on authentic Norwegian fare alongside Disney princesses at Epcot®.

3 Tusker House Restaurant
Appropriately dressed in safari garb, Donald Duck and friends join guests at this African-inspired restaurant in Disney's Animal Kingdom® Park.

4 1900 Park Fare
Have breakfast with Mary Poppins or a sit-down dinner with other Disney favorites at the Grand Floridian Resort.

5 Hollywood & Vine
You'll be joined by characters from the Disney Junior TV network at breakfast and lunch, making this a hot spot for tinier tots. Minnie and friends sometimes pop in for dinner.

6 Chef Mickey's
Mickey hosts American buffet breakfasts and dinners in Disney's Contemporary Resort.

7 Garden Grill Restaurant
This slowly revolving restaurant boasts a feast of farm-fresh foods and mealtime visits from Chip 'n' Dale.

8 The Crystal Palace
Meet Pooh and his pals for buffet breakfasts, lunches, and dinners in the Magic Kingdom®.

9 Café La Bamba
Characters from *Despicable Me: Minion Mayhem* turn up for breakfast.

10 Cape May Café
Join Goofy for a breakfast buffet at the Beach Club Resort.

TOP10 Places to Have a Drink

1 Lucky Leprechaun
A lively, welcoming Orlando institution with an Irish theme. It *(see p108)* offers a huge selection of beers, including all the Irish brews you could want, plus food. There is karaoke every night, live entertainment, and big-screen TVs showing major sporting events. It's a popular hangout with the locals.

2 California Grill Lounge
This is a fabulous place *(see p100)* to kick back, enjoy a bottle of wine, and watch the Magic Kingdom® fireworks. The secret is out, though, so arrive early for a table.

3 Jock Lindsey's Hangar Bar
MAP G2 ■ Disney Springs™ Landing ■ 407-939-6244
Stop in for a drink at this atmospheric 1940s Indiana Jones-inspired bar. The building is designed to look as if it were an old airplane hangar that, over time, turned into a favorite hang-out for the Society of Adventurers and Explorers. Strewn with artifacts and airplane parts, this charming bar serves up creatively named cocktails and tasty appetizers.

4 La Cava del Tequila
MAP G2 ■ Mexico Pavilion, Epcot® ■ 407-842-1132
In the midst of the bustling Mexico plaza in Epcot®, under the starlit sky, La Cava del Tequila offers over 200 types of tequila, plus mezcal,

Seating area at La Cava del Tequila

margaritas, Mexican beer and wine. To soak up the booze, there's a selection of tasty treats, such as guacamole and queso blanco with corn chips, or shrimp cocktail.

5 Rix Lounge
MAP G2 ■ Disney's Coronado Springs Resort ■ 407-939-2856
This sophisticated lounge boasts stories-high ceilings, billowing curtains, rich red and gold furnishings enhanced by soft lighting, and creatively designed seating spaces that make you feel as if you're at a high-end Vegas club, and not a Disney resort. Savor appetizers, new world wine, or creative martinis, margaritas, and mojitos at this trendy nightspot.

Swanky bar area at the Rix Lounge

6 Trader Sam's Grog Grotto and Tiki Terrace

MAP F1 ■ Disney's
Polynesian Village Resort
■ 407-939-3463

As if taken straight out of the Jungle Cruise (one of the park's most popular and long-standing rides), this whimsically themed lounge boasts a vintage tropical atmosphere. Drinks here are as wildly themed (some packing a powerful punch) as the lounge itself.

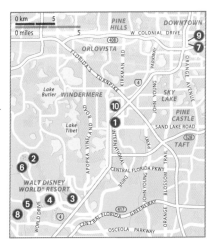

7 The Bösendorfer Lounge

Visitors can enjoy a drink or two along with soothing music at this classy lounge (see p122), after a show at the Dr. Phillips Center across the street. Live jazz features the Imperial Grand Bösendorfer Piano on Friday and Saturday nights.

8 Nomad Lounge

MAP G1 ■ Disney's Animal
Kingdom® ■ 407-939-3463

Located adjacent to Tiffins (see p101), this refreshing oasis serves up specialty cocktails and tasty small plates. The decor is themed around exploring the globe. After-dinner liqueurs include Bailey's Irish Cream, Tia Maria, and Amaretto di Saronno. Cap off the evening with an espresso or cappuccino after a long day enjoying the park.

9 The Courtesy

MAP P3 ■ 114 N. Orange
Ave ■ 407-450-2041

This speakeasy bar specializes in hand-crafted cocktails concocted using local and fresh ingredients; there's also a fine collection of absinthe, beer, and wine available to order. Its cozy ambience, and the friendly and knowledgeable staff, make for a thoroughly enjoyable evening. The bar gets very busy

so go early to avoid the crowds. The Courtesy also offers cocktail making classes on select Saturdays. Book in advance.

Chic interior at Velvet Bar

10 Velvet Bar

MAP E3 ■ Hard Rock Hotel,
5800 Universal Blvd ■ 407-503-2000

In the chic, swanky atmosphere of the Hard Rock Hotel at Universal Orlando Resort™, this high-end bar is definitely the place to see and be seen. Star sightings are not unheard of here, and it's widely considered to be one of the hottest nightspots in town. "Velvet Sessions" boast live performances by legendary rockers, served up alongside specially selected cocktails and beverages.

🔟 Places to Shop

1 Orlando International Premium Outlets

MAP U2 ▪ 4951 International Dr ▪ 407-352-9600 ▪ www.premium outlets.com

This 180-store mall offers upscale outlet stores such as Perry Ellis, Michael Kors, Lacoste, Coach, Kate Spade, Aeropostale, The Diamond Co., Movado, Bose, Victoria's Secret, Adidas, and Le Creuset.

Discounted shopping at Orlando International Premium Outlets

2 Mall at Millenia

MAP E4 ▪ 4200 Conroy Rd ▪ 407-363-3555 ▪ www.mallat millenia.com

Upscale and uptown, the Mall at Millenia contains luxury retailers including Tiffany & Co., Louis Vuitton, Neiman Marcus, and Jimmy Choo, as well as mid-price stores like Macy's, Pottery Barn, and Gap. Valet parking and currency exchange are available, and there's also a US Post Office in the mall, which is handy for mailing purchases home or sending gifts. Special events held here include fashion expos and inter-active children's activities. Central Florida's only IKEA store is also right across the road from here.

3 Orlando Vineland Premium Outlets

MAP F3 ▪ 8200 Vineland Ave ▪ 407-238-7787 ▪ www.premiumoutlets.com

This terrific 150-store complex is located just across I-4 from the east entrance of Disney World®. It boasts high-end designer outlets from Versace, DKNY, and Barney's New York, as well as a mix of popular brands, including Nike, Timberland, and Banana Republic.

4 Florida Mall

MAP E4 ▪ 8001 S. Orange Blossom Trail ▪ 407-851-6255 ▪ www.simon.com

Sure, it's a big enclosed suburban mall, but it's also one of the best in Central Florida, and hugely popular with visitors and locals. Stores include Armani Exchange, Vera Bradley, Coach, M&M's World, and more than 200 others.

5 Universal CityWalk™

MAP E3 ▪ Universal Orlando Resort™ ▪ 407-224-4233 ▪ www.universalorlando.com

Known for its clubs, restaurants, and entertainment venues, CityWalk™ also lays claim to a number of upscale

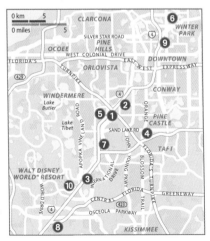

Stores line Universal CityWalk™

shops and boutiques. Browse casual resort wear at The Island Clothing Store, the latest in skate and surf wear at Quiet Flight Surf Shop, bright cotton clothing and accessories at Fresh Produce, and leather goods and jewelry at Fossil.

6 Park Avenue
This eight-block stretch of downtown Winter Park (see p125) retains an old-time feel. A canopy of live oak trees shades the brick-paved street, which is overlooked on one side by low buildings and flanked by relaxing Central Park. Many of the stores on this upscale avenue are independents, but there are some national chains too, such as Williams & Sonoma and Lilly Pulitzer. There's no food court, but the sidewalks are lined with places for lunch or dinner.

7 Pointe Orlando
MAP T4 ■ 9101 International Dr ■ 407-248-2838 ■ www.pointe orlando.com
Pointe Orlando is a shopping, dining, and entertainment complex. It offers something for everyone – a 20+ screen cinema, a WonderWorks entertainment center, BB King's Blues Club, a number of upscale restaurants, and more than 20 retail stores, including Victoria's Secret, Filthy Rich, Flow, and lots of specialty stores. The landscaped outdoor layout makes this a pleasant place for a shopping spree.

8 Celebration
This Disney-designed town and planned community (see p113), across I-4 to the southeast of Walt Disney World®, features a quaint little downtown district. Here a number of quality restaurants, a movie theater, a high-end hotel, and several small, one-of-a-kind shops and boutiques can be found lining Market Street.

9 Ivanhoe Row
MAP N3 ■ N. Orange Ave
This stretch of antique shops has thinned out in recent times due to rising rents, but there are still more than a dozen stores offering vintage linens, clothing, jewelry, and various collectables. Imported furniture from Bali and vintage LPs can also be found here.

10 Disney Springs™
Inspired by real Florida riverside towns, Disney's waterside shopping, entertainment, and dining district (see p95) offers a fantastic range of Disney-themed stores, stylish boutiques, and souvenir kiosks. Take a stroll and be awed with the choices, including The World of Disney, Once Upon A Toy, House of Blues® Company Store and the LEGO® Imagination Store. Town Center offers high-end shopping, with boutiques including Kate Spade, Coach, Free People, Lucky Brand, and Lacoste, among others. West Side, in addition to its restaurants and entertainment venues, also adds a few shops to the mix.

LEGO® sculpture at Disney Springs™

🔟 Orlando for Free

The serene Lake Eola Park at nighttime

1 Lake Eola Park

This Downtown park *(see p120)* features a beautiful lake and monthly farmers' markets, plus free concerts and outdoor theatrical productions in the warmer months.

2 Disney Springs™

Explore this recently redesigned area, divided into the Landing, the Marketplace, West Side, and Town Center. Filled with shops, restaurants, entertainment venues, and smaller attractions, Disney Springs™ *(see p95)* is a hub of activity both day and night. Free concerts are staged at various times. Strolling from area to area, and exploring the numerous shops and sites is a favorite pastime of park-goers in need of a break from the rides.

3 Universal CityWalk™

Acting as the entry point for Universal's theme parks, CityWalk™ *(see p82)* is filled from top to bottom with shops, restaurants, small attractions, and entertainment venues. People-watching is a favorite activity here, but there is also the occasional free concert, street performance, or live taping of a popular TV talk show. You can also ride the water taxis to the Universal resorts free of charge.

4 Harry P. Leu Gardens

Explore the beautiful and extensive gardens *(see p119)* at the Harry P. Leu Estate for free on the first Monday of select months.

Harry P. Leu Gardens

5 Music at Harbor Piazza, Loews Portofino Bay Hotel

"Musica della Notte" (Music of the Night) takes place every evening at Loews Portofino Bay Hotel's *(see p143)* Harbor Piazza. This charming celebration aims to capture the romance of Italy, showcasing classic opera and, on occasion, popera (a combination of pop and opera). Special themed nights include Romantico Night, Classico Night, and Italian Festival Night. Performances usually begin at sunset, if weather permits.

6 University of Central Florida Arboretum

4000 Central Florida Boulevard ▪ 407-823-3583 ▪ Open 9am–4pm daily

This arboretum has a maze of hiking trails through many distinctive ecological habitats, including a magnificent cypress dome, an oak hammock, and 32 acres (130,000 sq m) of pine flatwoods. Informative signage helps you identify various species.

7 Disney's BoardWalk

While the daytime is quiet, the night brings out carnival games and street performers. Other than activities along the BoardWalk (see p96) itself, you'll have a great view of the evening fireworks display at Epcot®.

8 Fort Christmas Historical Park

1300 N. Fort Christmas Rd ▪ 407-254-9310 ▪ Open winter: 8am–6pm daily (summer: to 8pm)

Built on Christmas Day, 1837, during the Second Seminole War, Fort Christmas has been re-created in this historical park. Guests can also visit Florida Cracker houses, a school, a sugar cane mill, and a museum.

Fort Christmas Historical Park

9 Grand Bohemian Gallery

A visit to this gallery (see p47) lets you enjoy Orlando's cultural side.

10 Kraft Azalea Gardens

MAP K4 ▪ 1364 Alabama Drive ▪ Open 8am–sunset daily

Located on the shore of Lake Maitland, this 5-acre (20,200-sq-m) garden has huge Cypress trees and bright azaleas.

TOP 10 BUDGET TIPS

The I-Ride Trolley

1 To travel up and down International Drive, take the I-Ride Trolley, which stops all along the bustling street, for just $2 per ride, or $5 for a day pass.

2 If you're not hungry enough for a full meal, order off the appetizer menu instead – portions in the theme parks are large.

3 Take advantage of the free transportation systems at Disney and Universal resorts. The schedules (see p132) are worth getting to grips with.

4 Eat your main meal at lunchtime or earlier than the usual dining times, when prices are often lower.

5 Purchase Universal® Orlando theme park tickets ahead of time online. This can often save you 10%, and sometimes even 20%, on gate prices.

6 Purchase multi-day theme park tickets, which are better value the longer you stay.

7 Watch for discounted room rates, free dining plans, and other promotional offers throughout the year. These can save you hundreds (or more).

8 Purchase the Disney Dining Plan (available to Disney resort guests), which works out much cheaper than purchasing all the equivalent meals separately.

9 Bring bottled water to the parks and refill them at the plentiful water fountains. Parks charge high prices for water, and it can add up to a big expense on a hot day.

10 Disney's Magical Express, an airport transfer service exclusive to Disney, is free to guests staying at a Walt Disney World® Resort. This can save a family of four up to $200.

🔟 Festivals and Events

1 Central Florida Fair
MAP C3 ▪ 4603 W. Colonial Dr
▪ 407-295-3247 ▪ Early Mar ▪ www.
centralfloridafair.com

This massive 19-day shindig takes place close to Downtown Orlando, but its cowboy attitude is a world away. The country-style attractions include carnival rides, livestock shows, country music, farming exhibits, and more fried food than you'll ever care to eat.

2 Winter Park Sidewalk Arts Festival
MAP C5 ▪ Park Ave, Winter Park
▪ 407-644-7207 ▪ Mid-Mar
▪ www.wpsaf.org

For three days, this prestigious outdoor festival sees hundreds of artists exhibit on sidewalk stalls. Traffic comes to a standstill as the crowds mill around.

3 Epcot® International Flower & Garden Festival
MAP G2 ▪ Epcot® ▪ 407-939-2273
▪ Mar–May ▪ www.disneyworld.com

This annual event features characters ingeniously created from topiary and flowers throughout the park. Everywhere you look, there are gardens filled with blooms of every shape, size, and color. The festival also features demonstrations, tours, and a series of outdoor concerts.

Toy Story at Epcot® International Flower & Garden Festival

4 Florida Film Festival
MAP K3 ▪ Enzian Theater, 1300 S. Orlando Ave, and other venues ▪ 407-629-1088 ▪ Apr
▪ www.floridafilmfestival.com

This 10-day film festival is packed with more than 180 features, documentaries, and shorts. Filmmakers introduce their works, and a few Hollywood names make guest appearances.

5 Orlando International Fringe Festival
Various venues ▪ 407-648-0077
▪ May ▪ www.orlandofringe.org

With more than 500 performances taking place over 14 days, the Fringe includes improvised comedy, drag shows, stand-up, and more. Inspired by the Edinburgh Fringe, this premier festival event draws enthusiastic local crowds.

6 Gay Days
Various venues ▪ 888-942-9329 or 407-896-8431 ▪ May–Jun
▪ www.gaydays.com

Gay Days is a week-long blowout of parties and theme park visits for more than 130,000 guests. By day, all visitors here wear a red t-shirt and mix in the parks; at night, parks and clubs are rented out as venues for evening raves. Many hotels also host Gay Days pool parties.

(7) Epcot® International Food & Wine Festival

MAP G2 ▪ Epcot® ▪ 407-939-2273
▪ Aug–Nov ▪ www.disneyworld.com
Along with demonstrations, tastings, and events, guests can purchase sample plates of foods from around the world at this international festival.

(8) IMMERSE – Creative City Project

MAP P3 ▪ Orange Ave ▪ Oct
▪ www.creativecityproject.com
More than 1,000 artists – musicians, dancers, visual artists, theatrical troupes, writers – take part in this annual two-day-and-night collaborative event in Downtown Orlando.

Performers at IMMERSE

(9) International Dragon Boat Festival

MAP D3 ▪ Bill Frederick Park at Turkey Lake ▪ Mid-Oct
This boat festival, steeped in Chinese folklore, sees more than 70 teams compete. There are 20 paddlers per vessel, with a drummer in the bow to keep the strokes in time. Visit the Asia Trend Cultural Expo to learn more about other Asian cultures.

(10) Festival of the Trees

MAP M3 ▪ Orlando Museum of Art ▪ 407-896-4231 ▪ Nov
Celebrate the spirit of the holiday season for nine days in November, when the museum (see p119) is transformed into a winter wonderland displaying beautifully decorated trees, holiday wreaths, vignettes, and candy-laden gingerbread houses.

TOP 10 ATTRACTION EVENTS

Mardi Gras at Universal

1 Walt Disney World® Marathon
Epcot® ▪ Jan
Runners partake in this 26.2-mile (42-km) race around the resort.

2 Mardi Gras at Universal
Universal Studios Florida™ ▪ Feb–Apr
The ultimate "Big Easy" party, with parades, music, and lots of beads.

3 Grad Bash
Universal Orlando Resort™ ▪ Apr
Live concerts, multiple dance parties, and thrill rides for seniors.

4 Rock the Universe
Universal Orlando Resort™ ▪ Sep
Universal's 2-night showcase of Christian rock music.

5 Halloween Horror Nights
Universal Studios Florida™ ▪ Sep–Nov
Universal is transformed into a ghoulish home for the undead.

6 Mickey's Not-So-Scary Halloween Party
Magic Kingdom® ▪ Sep–Oct
Trick-or-treat through the park for some ghostly family-appropriate fun.

7 Craft Beer Festival
Nov
More than 100 craft beers from various breweries are on offer on weekends.

8 Candlelight Processional
Epcot® World Showcase ▪ Nov–Dec
A celebrity narrator, along with a 50-piece orchestra and choir, tells the story of Christmas.

9 Mickey's Very Merry Christmas Party
Magic Kingdom® ▪ Nov–Dec
A festive parade complete with snow.

10 Grinchmas
Universal's Islands of Adventure™ ▪ Dec
Enjoy a live performance of *How the Grinch Stole Christmas* at Seuss Landing.

🔟 Day Trips South and West

1 Caladesi Island State Park

MAP B1 ■ 1 Causeway Blvd, Dunedin ■ 727 469 5918 ■ Ferry runs 10am–5pm daily ■ Open 8am to sunset ■ Adm

This 3-mile (5-km) island, accessible by ferry from Honeymoon Island, is a lovely retreat traversed by a nature trail. A ban on cars helps keep it much as it was a century ago. In season, beach areas are dotted with the tracks of loggerhead turtles that nest here.

Treasure Island Beach, the Gulf Coast

2 The Gulf Beaches

Florida's Gulf Coast is strewn with miles upon miles of white-sand, low-surf, and warm-water beaches stretching from Pinellas County (Clearwater Beach and St. Pete Beach among the many headliners) to Lee County (including Fort Myers Beach, Sanibel and Captiva Islands), on down to Collier County (Naples Beach and Marco Island).

3 Ybor City/Centro Ybor

MAP B1 ■ Seventh Ave, Tampa ■ www.ybor.org

The Latin heart of Tampa contains the Ybor City Museum State Park plus trendy art galleries and cafés. Take the opportunity to try a Cuban sandwich, and strong *café cubano* at the Columbia Restaurant, or to salsa and merengue into the small hours in one of the district's lively clubs.

4 Salvador Dali Museum

MAP B1 ■ 1 Dali Blvd, St. Petersburg ■ 727 823 3767 ■ Open 10am–5:30pm Fri–Wed, 10am–8pm Thu ■ www.thedali.org

One of the world's most comprehensive collections of Salvador Dali's work from 1914 to 1970 can be found at this world-class museum. The art on display includes oils, watercolors, and sculptures by the great Surrealist. There's also a café and an interesting outdoor space.

5 Florida Southern College

Located in Lakeland, 50 miles (80 km) southwest of Orlando, this private college's (see p64) architecture is impressive. In 1938, Frank Lloyd Wright was tasked with transforming a lakeside orange grove into a modern campus. The resulting 12 buildings became known as Child of the Sun, outlining Wright's belief that his buildings would inspire the college's students. His designs certainly impress visitors to the campus.

6 Busch Gardens

MAP B1 ▪ 3000 E. Busch Blvd, Tampa ▪ 813-987-5082 ▪ Hours vary seasonally ▪ Adm ▪ www.busch gardens.com

With world-class roller coasters, water rides, and numerous other attractions, this park is a close second to Universal's Islands of Adventure™ (see pp30–33). Roller coaster addicts rate the park's SheiKra ride very highly – it's a floorless 70-mph (120-km/h) coaster. Nature lovers will enjoy the animal interactions of the Jungala attraction and the truck ride through the plains of the Serengeti Safari. Ask about the free shuttle from Orlando for ticketholders.

7 Bok Tower Gardens

MAP B2 ▪ 1151 Tower Blvd, Lake Wales ▪ 863-676-1408 ▪ Open 8am–6pm daily ▪ Adm ▪ www.boktower gardens.org

This National Historic Landmark has nearly 250 acres (1 sq km) of grounds surrounding a 205-ft (62-m) bell tower and Mediterranean Revival mansion. The visitor center shows a video, and has a museum, café, and gift shop.

Bok Tower Gardens

Elephants, ZooTampa at Lowry Park

8 ZooTampa at Lowry Park

MAP B1 ▪ 1101 W. Sligh Ave, Tampa ▪ 813 935 8552 ▪ Open 9:30am–5pm daily ▪ Adm ▪ www. zootampa.org

Tampa's first zoo holds 1,300+ creatures, including Malayan tigers, African elephants, and Komodo dragons. It also serves as a rehabilitation center for injured manatees and as a sanctuary for Florida panthers and red wolves. Activities such as roller coaster rides, carousels, and a safari ride make for a fun-filled day.

9 Henry B. Plant Museum

MAP B1 ▪ 410 W. Kennedy Blvd, Tampa ▪ 813 254 1891 ▪ Open 10am–5pm Tue–Sat, noon–5pm Sun ▪ Adm ▪ www.plantmuseum.com

In the late 1800s, railroad magnate Henry B. Plant built an opulent Moorish palace in the swamps of Tampa, attracting tourists and celebrities alike. Now part of the University of Tampa, this museum honors the life and times of Plant. Take a tour through its restored rooms.

10 Florida Aquarium

MAP B1 ▪ 701 Channelside Dr, Tampa ▪ 813 273 4000 ▪ Open 9:30am–5pm daily ▪ Adm ▪ www. flaquarium.org

Florida's native species are just a fraction of more than 10,000 animals and plants here. Wetlands, bays, coral reefs, and their inhabitants are featured in several galleries. You can watch divers feed marine creatures.

Day Trips North and East

1 Kennedy Space Center Visitor Complex

This well-conceived monument (see pp40–43) to America's space program impresses visitors with mammoth exhibits, such as the Saturn V Rocket, and smaller items, such as old space suits. Bus tours are a good way to take in the installations.

Kennedy Space Center Visitor Complex

2 Daytona Beach
MAP A3 ■ Tourist info: 386-255-0415

During the annual Spring Break, this legendary beach (just 90 minutes from Orlando along I-4) is the destination for thousands of vacationing college students, who drink and party until they drop. But sun and fun isn't all that's offered. Beach Street is lined with shops, restaurants, and clubs; and of course, there's also the Daytona Speedway, home to the Daytona 500 and other NASCAR races.

3 New Smyrna Beach
MAP A3

Just south of Daytona Beach, New Smyrna is a smaller, calmer town that lacks Daytona's party scene. The white sand beach is picture perfect – but as at Daytona, cars share the space with sunworshipers. For food, the place to go is JB's Fish Camp, a raucous and friendly shack beside Mosquito Lagoon, serving some of the state's tastiest fish, seafood, and key lime pie.

4 Sebastian Inlet
MAP B3

Located 15 miles (24 km) south of Melbourne, Sebastian Inlet's waves draw surfers from near and far, with several major competitions held here each year. The pristine white-sand beach only adds to the appeal. It's also a good saltwater fishing spot, while history buffs will enjoy a walk through the McLarty Treasure Museum and the Sebastian Fishing Museum.

5 Mount Dora
MAP A2 ■ Tourist info: 352-383-2165

Just 25 miles (40 km) from Orlando, charming Mount Dora seems plucked from the 1950s. The cozy downtown is unmarred by strip malls or chain stores. Instead, the local industry is antiques, with dozens of small shops on and around Donnelly Street as well as Reninger's Antique & Flea Markets on the edge of town. Train buffs can enjoy a guided tour ride on the trolley, and Lake Dora offers plenty of boating opportunities.

Cocoa Beach's pier offers spectacular views

6 Cassadaga Spiritualist Camp

MAP A2 ■ Cassadaga Camp Bookstore: 1112 Stevens St ■ Open 10am–6pm Mon–Sat, 11:30am–5pm Sun ■ 386-228-2880 ■ www.cassadaga.org

Buried in the woods near exit 114 off I-4, tiny Cassadaga was founded more than 100 years ago as a community of clairvoyants, mediums, and healers. Resident spiritualists promote the science, philosophy, and the religion of Spiritualism; offer contacts with the deceased in the Spirit World; and provide healing services for the body, mind, and spirit.

7 Merritt Island National Wildlife Refuge

This 140,000-acre (567-sq-km) wildlife sanctuary *(see pp38–9)* (the second largest in Florida) has more federally endangered species than any other refuge in the United States. A 7-mile (11-km) driving tour with shaded boardwalks weaves through lush pine and oak hammocks.

Alligator on Merritt Island

8 Cocoa Beach
MAP B3

Just 60 miles (96 km) east of I-4 via the Beachline Expressway, Cocoa Beach is the seashore closest to Orlando. The lengthy stretch of sand and the surf are the reasons visitors flock to this laidback town. While the coastline may be pretty, the town is less so (apart from the lovely Cocoa Village near Hwy 1).

9 St. Augustine

This welcoming seaside city bears influences from the Spanish Conquistadors, the Timucua, and even the British – there are over 60 historic sites, including the Castillo de San Marco and Fort Matanzas. Adding to the charm of the historic district, and set along the brick-lined streets, are independently owned restaurants and quaint boutiques, with live music often filling the air. Explore by horse-drawn carriage, or a hop-on hop-off trolley tour. The lighthouse is said to be one of the most haunted sites in the US.

10 Amelia Island

Set off the northeastern coast, this pristine barrier island offers 13 miles (21 km) of sugary white-sand beaches, a charming historic district filled with boutiques and bistros, and an array of activities to keep you busy, including fishing, boating, golfing, hiking, and biking along the island trails.

Orlando
Area by Area

Downtown Orlando at dusk,
viewed across Lake Eola

TOP10 Walt Disney World® Resort and Lake Buena Vista

There was just one drawback to California's Disneyland®, Walt Disney's first theme park, which opened in 1955: there was no space around the park in which to expand. Following an aerial tour of Central Florida in 1965, Disney began to buy large tracts of land. At the time, this patch of the state was mainly cow pastures, citrus groves, and swamps. Today, the 47-sq-mile (121-sq-km) Walt Disney World® Resort is a self-governing entity containing four major theme parks, two water parks, several smaller attractions, and many hotels and resorts, which spill over into the adjoining Lake Buena Vista area. For some of the 50 million guests who visit annually, it's a once-in-a-lifetime vacation, but many return time and again.

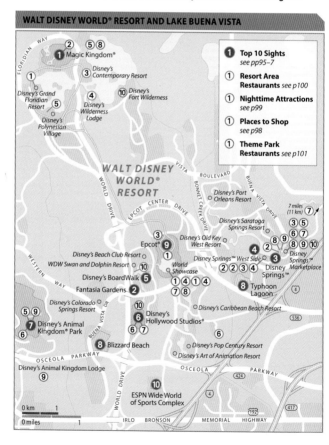

WALT DISNEY WORLD® RESORT AND LAKE BUENA VISTA

- **1** Top 10 Sights *see pp95–7*
- **1** Resort Area Restaurants *see p100*
- **1** Nighttime Attractions *see p99*
- **1** Places to Shop *see p98*
- **1** Theme Park Restaurants *see p101*

Parade through Main Street U.S.A.® in the Magic Kingdom®

1 Magic Kingdom®

Who's the leader of the theme-park pack? Disney's first Florida park (see pp12–15) is the most popular in the US.

2 Fantasia Gardens and Winter Summerland Miniature Golf

Fantasia Gardens: MAP G2; 407-560-4582; open 10am–11pm daily; adm ■ Winter Summerland: MAP G1; 407-560-3000; open 10am–11pm daily; adm

Orlando in general and Walt Disney World® Resort in particular have some great golf courses (see pp62–3), but not everyone likes to take the game so seriously, or has the makings of a pro. These two miniature golf courses offer a total of 72 holes of putting fun. Inspired by the classic

Miniature golf at Winter Summerland

Disney cartoon *Fantasia*, Fantasia Gardens' 18 holes have an animal theme. Located near Disney's Hollywood Studios®, it's the more forgiving of the two courses, and so the better choice for young kids or beginners. Winter Summerland is a scale model of a full-size course, complete with bunkers, water hazards, frustrating putting greens, and holes that are up to 75 ft (23 m) long. Here you can choose between the winter and summer themed courses.

3 Disney Springs™
MAP G2 ■ 407-939-6244 ■ www.disneysprings.com

With specially created waterways, bubbling springs (hence the name), and themed neighborhoods, this shopping, dining, and entertainment district is an attraction in itself. Each neighborhood has its own complement of stores and eating places, but Town Center boasts high-end retailers along with a number of signature restaurants. The Marketplace is the most family-friendly area, with a variety of kid's shops, the occasional free concert, and casual counter-service restaurants. The Landing offers more upscale dining, with THE BOATHOUSE® (see p77) among the notable restaurants. Westside has a cluster of entertainment venues, along with some eclectic shops.

Entrance to Splitsville Luxury Lanes™

4 Splitsville Luxury Lanes™

MAP G2 ▪ Disney Springs™ West Side ▪ 407-938-7467 ▪ Hours vary ▪ Adm

This upscale bowling alley in Disney Springs™ is spread across two levels and an area of 50,000 sq ft (4,645 sq m). Teams have access to 30 luxury lanes, and unique food specialties are served right by the lane table – choices include a variety of pizzas and drinks, along with gluten-free sushi. Other than this, there is an outdoor patio area as well as large-screen TVs and pool tables.

HIDDEN MICKEYS

Hidden Mickeys started many years ago as a joke among park designers. Today they're a Disney tradition. They're images of the world's most famous mouse: silhouettes of Mickey's ears, his head and ears, or his whole body, semi-hidden throughout the parks and resorts. They can be anywhere: in the landscaping, in the murals you pass while waiting in ride lines, and even overhead, for example on the Earffel Tower in Disney's Hollywood Studios®. See how many you can spot (www.hiddenmickeys.org).

5 Disney's BoardWalk

MAP W2 ▪ 2101 Epcot Resorts Blvd ▪ 407-939-6244

Disney's BoardWalk is designed to reflect the splendor of the original boardwalks set along the Atlantic seaboard in the 19th century. Adjacent to the Victorian-style Disney's BoardWalk Inn & Villas, and only a short distance from the Swan & Dolphin and Disney's Beach & Yacht Club resorts, this popular dining and entertainment district is constantly bustling with activity. Wrapping around Crescent Lake, it boasts a number of Disney's most popular restaurants, such as the famed Flying Fish (see p100). Completing the nostalgic scene is an ice cream shop, pizza window, and at night expect to see street performers and boardwalk games added to the mix. Just across the lake is Epcot®, and the nearby lawn is a perfect spot for sitting to watch its nighttime fireworks display. Surrey bikes are also popular here, with seating for 2, 4, or 6 – you can bike all the way around the lake and back.

6 Disney's Hollywood Studios®

A park (see pp20–21) that combines front-of-house fun with behind-the-scenes explanation. It is also home to some of Disney's most intense thrill rides and plenty of Star Wars experiences.

7 Disney's Animal Kingdom® Park

Disney's fourth Orlando park (see pp22–3) is a place where exotic animals roam within a variety of far-flung landscapes. Intrepid adventurers will find lots to do here.

Lion, Disney's Animal Kingdom® Park

8 Water Parks

Typhoon Lagoon: MAP G2; 407-560-4141; adm ▪ Blizzard Beach: MAP G1; 407-560-3400; adm

Walt Disney World® has two water parks (see pp56–7). Typhoon Lagoon is designed to resemble a beach resort devastated by a tropical storm, can hold more than 7,000 people at once, and has plenty of rides and attractions. Blizzard Beach imagines a melted ski resort. Whatever the theme, both parks have similar features: long drops to build up speed and darkened tubes to confuse you before spilling you into a wading pool below. The parks have seasonal hours, so call to check.

Lazy River at Typhoon Lagoon

9 Epcot®

Walt Disney's guys knew a park had to appeal to curious adults and techno kids. Epcot® (see pp16–19), as a result, is a celebration of technology and culture.

10 ESPN Wide World of Sports Complex

MAP G2 ▪ 407-939-1500 ▪ Opening times vary ▪ Adm

Disney's sports complex is the spring training home of Major League baseball's Atlanta Braves (Feb–Mar) and minor league baseball's Orlando Rays, a farm team for the Tampa Bay Devil Rays (Apr–Sep). It's also a winter home for basketball's Harlem Globetrotters. Other facilities in the complex, which

WALT DISNEY

Walter Elias Disney was just 26 years old when his most famous cartoon character, Mickey Mouse, was introduced in the film Steamboat Willie (1928). Despite escalating success in the film world as he embraced first sound then Technicolor, Disney had his sights set on more than just animation. He was the man who created the theme park, which he envisaged as a kind of 3-D movie, where each individual could spin his or her own story in a totally safe, controlled, and upbeat environment. His first, California's Disneyland® Park, was the perfect vehicle for bringing Disney's clean-living family values and nostalgia to the masses. It was also the only one of his parks that came to fruition before his death in 1966 from lung cancer, 11 years after it opened.

is used for all kinds of amateur sports, include a fitness center; basket-ball, volleyball, and tennis courts; softball, soccer, and lacrosse fields; a martial-arts venue; and a golf driving range. ESPN Wide World of Sports Complex is also the home of the NFL Experience. There is an extreme sports area catering for skateboarders, in-line skaters, and cyclists, which is also open for special events.

Athlete at ESPN Sports Complex®

Places to Shop

1 House of Good Fortune
MAP G2 ■ China Pavilion, World Showcase, Epcot®

Here's an excellent source for all things Asian, from jade figurines to silk robes, and inlaid mother-of-pearl furnishings to wind chimes.

2 Pop Gallery
MAP G2 ■ Disney Springs™ West Side

Original works of art are showcased and sold here, including sculptures, paintings, and glassware, along with an array of unique, trendy gift items.

Sculptures at The LEGO® Store

3 The LEGO® Store
MAP G2 ■ Disney Springs™ Marketplace

Kids love the play area, which has enough LEGO® pieces to build almost anything. Inside, the cash registers sing as parents buy the latest sets of bricks.

4 Mitsukoshi Department Store
MAP G2 ■ Japan Pavilion, World Showcase, Epcot®

An amazing selection of kimonos, samurai swords, bonsais, Japanese Disneyana, and kites is sold here.

5 Twenty Eight & Main
MAP G2 ■ Disney Springs™ Marketplace

A small boutique offering a selection of vintage-inspired gentlemen's clothing and accessories.

6 Basin
MAP G2 ■ Disney Springs™ Marketplace

Shelves, buckets, and cubbies overflow with colorful bath balls, scented soaps, and natural skin-care products in this great-smelling store.

7 Art of Disney
MAP G2 ■ Disney Springs™ Marketplace

This one-of-a-kind gallery is filled with Disney sculptures, animation cels (celluloid sheets used for films), and other collectibles.

8 Once Upon a Toy
MAP G2 ■ Disney Springs™ Marketplace

Step back in time for old-style toys like Lincoln Logs and Mr. Potato Head, progressing via a build-your-own *Star Wars* light saber to modern games.

9 Tren-D
MAP G2 ■ Disney Springs™ Marketplace

Stylish clothes and accessories, such as organic loungewear, embroidered bags, jeweled sunglasses, and creations by cutting-edge designers.

10 World of Disney®
MAP G2 ■ Disney Springs™ Marketplace

The Disney store to beat all stores – over 51,000 sq ft (4,738 sq m) brimming with clothing, jewelry, toys, and souvenirs, plus the Bibiddi Bobiddi salon for all aspiring princes and princesses.

World of Disney® store

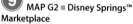

Nighttime Attractions

Fireworks at IllumiNations

① IllumiNations: Reflections of Earth

MAP G2 ■ World Showcase Lagoon, Epcot® ■ 407 828 0999 ■ Adm

A nightly explosion of lasers, fireworks, and fountains over the lagoon is set to music, celebrating world culture in a unique fashion.

② AMC® Disney Springs™ 24

MAP G2 ■ Disney Springs™ West Side ■ 407 939 5277

Twenty-four screens show the latest box office hits. There's also a massive ETX auditorium and several Fork & Screen® dine-in theaters.

③ Splitsville Luxury Lanes

MAP G2 ■ Disney Springs™ West Side ■ 407 938 7467 ■ Adm

A vintage 1950s-themed bowling alley complex (see p96), with several bars and restaurants, as well as 30 high-tech lanes.

④ House of Blues®

MAP G2 ■ Disney Springs™ West Side ■ 407 934 2583 ■ Adm

One of Orlando's best venues (see p68) for live music, hosting a wide variety of acts in various genres.

⑤ Happily Ever After

MAP F1 ■ Magic Kingdom®

The skies above Cinderella Castle are sprinkled with twinkling fireworks set to music and a story about wishes coming true.

⑥ Pandora – The World of Avatar

Disney's imagineers bring to life the sights of Pandora (from James Cameron's movie, *Avatar*) here (see p96). This mythical land becomes a glowing wonderland at night.

⑦ Fantasmic!

MAP G2 ■ Disney's Hollywood Studios® ■ 407 824 4321

Featuring a cast of favorite characters, this evening show is set in a huge outdoor theater with a stage surrounded by water.

⑧ Electrical Water Pageant

MAP G2 ■ Seven Seas Lagoon, Bay Lake, Magic Kingdom®

A colorful parade of illuminated creatures atop floating barges that ply the waters in front of the Magic Kingdom® resorts.

⑨ Discovery Island® Carnivale

MAP G2 ■ Disney's Animal Kingdom® ■ 407 824 4321

This colorful cavalcade of stilt walkers, dancers, and musicians performs on the streets at dusk to create a dance party reminiscent of spring celebrations around the world.

⑩ Hoop-Dee-Doo Musical Revue

MAP F1 ■ Disney's Fort Wilderness Resort ■ 407 939 3463 ■ 4, 6:15 & 8pm nightly

This show (see p74) combines an all-you-can-eat dinner with Country & Western dancing, singing, and comedy.

See map on p94 ←

Resort Area Restaurants

1 Victoria & Albert's
MAP F1 ▪ Disney's Grand Floridian Resort & Spa ▪ 407-824-1089 ▪ Pre-arrange vegetarian entrées ▪ No kids' menu ▪ $$$

This romantic gem *(see p76)* has an international menu served by a pair of attentive servers who treat guests like royalty.

2 T-REX™
MAP G2 ▪ Disney Springs™ ▪ 407-828-8739 ▪ $$

This dinosaur-themed café *(see p78)* serves American fare in an interactive setting. There are also a variety of hands-on discovery zones.

Exterior of T-REX™

3 California Grill
MAP F1 ▪ Disney's Contemporary Resort ▪ 407-824-1576 ▪ $$$

This vegetarian-friendly restaurant *(see p77)* serves delicious California cuisine in a romantic 15th-floor space.

4 Whispering Canyon
MAP F1 ▪ Disney's Wilderness Lodge ▪ 407-824-3200 ▪ $$

Sample hearty Western fare at this charming family-friendly restaurant *(see p78)*. The menu has a good range of kid-friendly options.

5 'Ohana
MAP F1 ▪ Disney's Polynesian Village Resort ▪ 407-939-3463 ▪ $$$

The specialty at 'Ohana *(see p79)* is the skewer service – meat, vegetarian, and seafood. Games, storytelling, and hula dancing accompany the all-you-can-eat Hawaiian-style dinner.

6 Bull & Bear Steakhouse
MAP G1 ▪ 14200 Bonnet Creek Ln ▪ 407-597-5500 ▪ Dinner only ▪ No kids' menu ▪ Pre-arrange vegetarian entrées ▪ $$$

Modeled after the original in New York, this restaurant *(see p76)* in the Waldorf Astoria has a high-end menu and impeccable service.

7 VIVO Italian Kitchen™
MAP T1 ▪ CityWalk™ ▪ 407-224-3663 ▪ $$$

The authentic Italian dinner choices here *(see p76)* are accompanied by vintage wines. Enjoy Chicken *picatta*, pastas, veal parmigiano, and linguine and clams in a comfortable cucina setting.

8 THE BOATHOUSE®
MAP G2 ▪ Disney Springs™ ▪ 407-824-3200 ▪ $$$

Meat and seafood entrees and appetizers are on offer at this themed restaurant *(see p77)*, where fine dining gets a nautical flavor. You can also take a trip on one of the Dream Boats™ from the '30s, '40s, and '50s.

9 Morimoto Asia
MAP G2 ▪ Disney Springs™ ▪ 407-939-6686 ▪ $$

Experience the finest in modern Pan-Asian cuisine here *(see p76)* as envisioned by chef Morimoto. Indulge in sushi, ribs, and other specialities from China, Japan and Korea.

10 Todd English's bluezoo
MAP G2 ▪ Dolphin Hotel, 1500 Epcot Resorts Blvd, Lake Buena Vista ▪ 407-934-1111 ▪ $$$

At this underwater-themed restaurant *(see p77)*, diners savour the locally-sourced seafood, plus tender chicken, beef, and pork dishes.

Theme Park Restaurants

① Via Napoli Ristorante e Pizzeria
MAP G2 ▪ Italy Pavilion, Epcot®
▪ 407-939-3463 ▪ $$

Authentic pizzas are made with ingredients from Italy in giant wood-burning ovens at this wonderful family-style restaurant (see p79).

Cinderella's Royal Table

② Cinderella's Royal Table
MAP F1 ▪ Magic Kingdom®
▪ 407-939-3463 ▪ Pre-arrange vegetarian entrées ▪ No alcohol ▪ $$$

Meet the princesses and Fairy Godmother while dining at this lavish eatery (see p79) inside Cinderella's castle. It's advisable to reserve ahead.

③ Coral Reef Restaurant
MAP G2 ▪ Living Seas Pavilion, Epcot® ▪ 407-939-3463 ▪ $$$

Enjoy seafood, meat, and vegetarian dishes on the seasonal menu here (see p78) against a fabulous backdrop of a living coral reef.

④ Le Cellier Steakhouse
MAP G2 ▪ Canadian Pavilion, Epcot® ▪ 407-939-1947 ▪ $$$

Inspired by the wine cellars of a grand château, stone arches and candle sconces set the tone here. Dine on prime meats, seafood, and poutine.

⑤ Tiffins
MAP G1 ▪ Disney's Animal Kingdom® ▪ 407-939-3463 ▪ $$$

This beautiful eatery is designed to resemble a vintage adventurers' club, with an elegant flair. The three dining rooms have exotic Asian and African decor, and the menu takes you on an international culinary expedition.

PRICE CATEGORIES

For a three-course meal for one, a glass of house wine, and all unavoidable extra charges including tax.

$ under $30 $$ $30–60 $$$ over $60

⑥ Sci-Fi Dine-In Theater Restaurant
MAP G2 ▪ Disney's Hollywood Studios® ▪ 407-939-3463 ▪ $$

All-American cuisine is on offer at this drive-in "theater" (see p78), where you can watch sci-fi movie clips from a car-shaped booth or table.

⑦ San Angel Inn
MAP G2 ▪ Mexico Pavilion, Epcot® ▪ 407-939-3463 ▪ $$$

Try mole poblano (chicken with spices and chocolate) or beef with black beans and fried plantain at this massive Mexican eatery.

⑧ Rose & Crown Pub and Dining Room
MAP G2 ▪ UK Pavilion, Epcot® ▪ 407-939-3463 ▪ Pre-arrange vegetarian entrées ▪ $$

A British-style pub offering staples such as bangers and mash, rib with Yorkshire pudding, and Cornish pasties.

⑨ Boma – Flavors of Africa
MAP G1 ▪ Disney's Animal Kingdom Lodge ▪ 407-939-1947 ▪ $$$

Enjoy an African dinner buffet at this restaurant (see p79) – one of Disney's most popular – where the tables are made from huge tree trunks. There's also a less exotic children's buffet.

⑩ 50's Prime Time Café
MAP G2 ▪ Disney's Hollywood Studios® ▪ 407-939-5277 ▪ $$

Watch '50s kitsch and vintage TV reruns here (see p78) as you dine on classic American comfort food – meatloaf, pot roast, and fried chicken.

See map on p94 ←

TOP 10 International Drive Area

International Drive is a brash and busy 10-mile (16-km) parkway boasting three major theme parks, countless smaller attractions, and the USA's second-largest convention center – with Universal's theme parks and entertainment complex right nearby. Added to the mix are hundreds of hotels and resorts catering to all budgets, shopping malls and outlet stores, and themed, casual, and fast-food restaurants. As a package, it is a frenetic zone, which, despite its neon signs and visual overload, has become a serious competitor to Walt Disney World®, appealing to visitors who prefer to stay out of the clutches of Mickey and get a bit closer to Harry Potter.

INTERNATIONAL DRIVE AREA

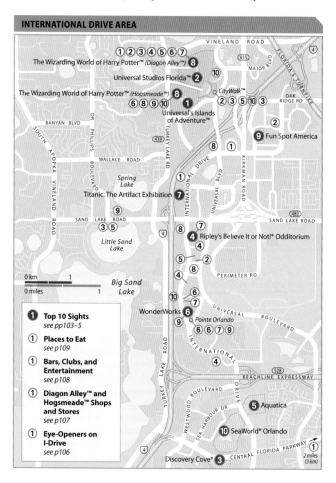

- ❶ **Top 10 Sights**
  see pp103–5
- ① **Places to Eat**
  see p109
- ① **Bars, Clubs, and Entertainment**
  see p108
- ① **Diagon Alley™ and Hogsmeade™ Shops and Stores**
  see p107
- ① **Eye-Openers on I-Drive**
  see p106

The Wizarding World of Harry Potter™ (Diagon Alley™)
Universal Studios Florida™
The Wizarding World of Harry Potter™ (Hogsmeade™)
Universal's Islands of Adventure™
CityWalk™
Fun Spot America
Titanic: The Artifact Exhibition
Ripley's Believe It or Not!® Odditorium
WonderWorks
Pointe Orlando
Aquatica
SeaWorld® Orlando
Discovery Cove®

0 km   1
0 miles   1

2 miles
(3 km)

Universal's Islands of Adventure™

1 Universal's Islands of Adventure™

Spiderman, The Hulk, Dr. Seuss, and the dinosaurs of Jurassic Park rule here *(see pp30–33)* – with wild rides dedicated to each.

2 Universal Studios Florida™

Part studio and part attraction, the movie-themed rides and shows here *(see pp26–9)* really let visitors step inside the motion pictures.

3 Discovery Cove®

MAP T6 ■ 6000 Discovery Cove Way ■ 407-370-1280 ■ Open 9am–5pm daily ■ Adm

You might be in land-locked Orlando, but you can still fulfill those tropical island fantasies of snorkeling over coral reefs if you check in to Discovery Cove® *(see p56)*. Visitors flock here for the white-sand beaches, snorkeling opportunities in fresh and salt-water lagoons, and relaxed beach-resort vibe. Admission is not cheap (largely because there are never more than 1,000 visitors daily), but you get almost everything you need for the day thrown in, including sun block, lunch, and snorkel gear, as well as a 7-day pass to SeaWorld®. Kids might miss the thrill rides, but they will not be short of things to do.

4 Ripley's Believe It or Not!® Odditorium

MAP T3 ■ 8201 International Dr ■ 407-363-4418 ■ Open 9am–midnight daily ■ Adm

If you're a fan of the bizarre, you'll love Ripley's. This worldwide chain of attractions displays the unbelievable finds of Robert Ripley's 40 years of adventures, the reports of which were published in more than 300 newspapers and read by more than 80 million people. The Orlando branch *(see p52)* has 16 themed galleries with over 600 exhibits and artifacts, such as a full-scale model of a 1907 Silver Ghost Rolls Royce (with moving engine parts) built out of 1,016,711 matchsticks and 63 pints (36 l) of glue; a wild spinning vortex tunnel; a flute made of human bones; a mosaic of the *Mona Lisa* made of toast; shrunken heads; a five-legged cow; and a portrait of Van Gogh made from 3,000 postcards.

Entrance to Ripley's Believe It or Not!® Odditorium

I-RIDE TROLLEY

One of the best things about I-Drive itself is the tourist-oriented I-Ride Trolley (see p132), which offers an easy way to see some of the area's oddities and its high-density visual overload. It is also an excellent and extremely cheap way to get around this part of town, while avoiding the need to get involved in fighting I-Drive's frustratingly heavy traffic, or walking any distance in the intense heat. There are 78 stops on the circuit, serving all the local major attractions, shopping malls, hotels, and restaurants.

5 Aquatica®

MAP U5 ▪ 5800 **Water Play Way, International Dr** ▪ 888-500-5447 ▪ **Open 10am–5pm, extended seasonal hours** ▪ **Adm**

SeaWorld®'s eco-themed water park, just across from SeaWorld® itself, makes a big splash with families and thrill seekers alike. It combines wild slides and rides, including an eight-person racing slide, with a number of tot-friendly options. The park has a whimsical South Pacific setting, which makes the perfect backdrop for up-close encounters with the park's wilder inhabitants, including brightly colored tropical fish, macaws, and African Spurred Tortoises. A stretch of white-sand sits adjacent to giant wave pools, while a winding river takes riders bobbing along the waterways of Loggerhead Lane. You can also rent cabanas in various sizes in advance.

6 WonderWorks

MAP T4 ▪ Pointe Orlando, 9067 International Dr ▪ 407-351-8800 ▪ Open 9am–midnight daily ▪ Adm

You can't miss this attraction (see p52) from the outside: it looks as though a classical building has landed upside down on top of a warehouse. Inside, there are 85 hands-on exhibits. Highlights include an earthquake simulator; a Bridge of Fire, where you can literally experience the hair-raising effects of 250,000 watts of static electricity; and Virtual Hoops, which uses some of the latest cinema technology to put you on TV to play basketball against one of the NBA's top players. You can also try virtual hang gliding, which sends you soaring like a bird through the

Astronaut costume at WonderWorks

Walkabout Waters, whimsical rain fortress at Aquatica®

Grand Canyon, and WonderCoaster, which challenges your roller coaster-designing skills and then your nerve to ride your creation in a simulator. WonderWorks also runs a laser-tag venue and a twice-nightly magic show, both of which cost extra.

Wintertime at The Wizarding World of Harry Potter™

⑦ Titanic: The Artifact Exhibition
MAP T3 ▪ 7324 International Dr ▪ 407-248-1166 ▪ Open 11am–10pm daily ▪ Adm

This exhibit's (see p53) 200 artifacts include a life jacket and an old deck chair, both recovered from the wreckage of the fateful liner, as well as the *Titanic*'s second-class passenger list. The attraction also has full-scale re-creations of some of the ship's interior, including its grand staircase, as well as memorabilia from three major *Titanic* movies – including one of the costumes worn by Leonardo DiCaprio. Actors in period garb play out events that occurred on the ill-fated voyage, telling the story of the White Star Line's supposedly unsinkable ship. Most of the artifacts came out of private collections in both the United Kingdom and the USA.

SEAWORLD CONTROVERSY

SeaWorld® has a rehabilitation program of rescuing stranded marine animals and, whenever possible, releasing them back into the wild. However, less positive aspects of SeaWorld® have come to light since the release of the 2013 documentary film *Blackfish*, which questioned the ethics of keeping killer whales in captivity. In 2016, SeaWorld® announced it would end its controversial orca whale breeding and performance program, but the park has come under strong criticism, seeing a downturn in public opinion and a drop in visitor numbers.

⑧ The Wizarding World of Harry Potter™

The addition of Hogsmeade™ to Universal's Islands of Adventure™ and Diagon Alley™ to Universal Studios Florida™ – the two linked by the Hogwarts™ Express – has cast its own spell over visitors, making Universal's parks (see pp34–5) more popular than ever.

⑨ Fun Spot America
MAP U2 ▪ 5500 Fun Spot Way ▪ 407-363-3867 ▪ Open 2pm–midnight, with extended seasonal and weekend hours

This arcade/amusement park (see p53) has something for everyone, with four go-kart tracks, two giant roller coasters, and the world's biggest SkyCoaster. There are bumper boats and cars, a Ferris wheel, arcade games, and a kid zone that has swings, a train, spinning tea cups, and flying bears.

⑩ SeaWorld® Orlando
MAP F3 ▪ 7007 Sea World Dr ▪ 888-800-5447 ▪ Open at least 9am–6pm daily ▪ Adm

While home to some of the wildest rides in all of Orlando (Mako, Manta, and Kraken), the majority of the park is dedicated to life under the sea. With exhibits dedicated to sharks, penguins, whales, manatees, and more, this park is unlike any other around. Its grounds are meticulously landscaped, with towering palm trees, a central lake, and blooming flowers at every turn.

See map on p102

Eye-Openers on I-Drive

Four Points by Sheraton Orlando Studio City

MAP T2 ▪ 5905 International Dr

This distinctive 21-story circular hotel has a huge globe sitting on top.

Madame Tussauds

MAP T3 ▪ 8401 International Dr ▪ 866-630-8315 ▪ Open 10am–10pm daily

Celebrity waxworks range from HM Queen Elizabeth II to Marilyn Monroe, and just about everyone in between.

3 **Hollywood Drive-In Golf**

MAP E3 ▪ 6000 Universal Blvd, Universal® Orlando ▪ 407-224-4233 ▪ Open 9am–2am daily

Two fun 1950s-B-movie-inspired mini-golf courses, with a graveyard and flying saucer theme and hilarious sound effects.

4 **King's Bowl**

MAP T3 ▪ 8255 S. International Dr ▪ 407-363-0200 ▪ Open 11am–2am daily

There are 22 bowling lanes over several levels on offer here, along with two full bars, a full service restaurant, and 60 giant TVs.

5 **ICON Orlando™**

MAP T3 ▪ 8401 International Dr ▪ 866-228-6438 ▪ Open 10am–10pm daily

Rising some 400 ft (122 m) above I-Drive, this giant wheel offers a bird's-eye view of the city as it slowly revolves.

6 **ICEBAR**

There's always something cool happening at this frozen cocktail bar (see p108), from karaoke and swing dance lessons to DJs.

7 **Ripley's Believe It or Not®! Odditorium**

This place (see p103) is built to look as if one of Florida's sinkholes opened and nearly swallowed the building.

8 **iFLY Orlando**

MAP T2 ▪ 6805 Visitors Cir ▪ 407-903-1150 ▪ Open 10am–9pm daily

A visit to this futuristic blue and purple building (see p53), gives you the opportunity to experience the sensation of flying in a virtual sky-diving experience.

9 **WonderWorks**

As the marketing story goes, a tornado picked up this four-story building (see p104) and sent it crashing upside down on top of a 1930s-era brick warehouse. Silly perhaps, but it stops traffic.

10 **Air Florida Helicopters**

MAP T4 ▪ 8990 International Dr ▪ 407-354-1400 ▪ Open 9:30am–8pm daily

With flights starting at just $20 (plus $4 for fuel) per person, there's no reason not to take this panoramic trip over the city.

ICON Orlando™ lit up at night

Diagon Alley™ and Hogsmeade™ Shops and Stores

1 **Weasleys' Wizard Wheezes™**

MAP T1 ■ Diagon Alley™

Whether you're shopping for skiving snackboxes, extendable ears, or love potions, you're sure to find something to your liking at this unique little joke shop.

2 **Borgin and Burkes™**

MAP T1 ■ Diagon Alley™

Down crooked Nocturn Alley, just off Diagon Alley™, this shop with dusty windows is filled with items infused with dark magic – including the hand of glory and poisonous potions.

3 **Magical Menagerie™**

MAP T1 ■ Diagon Alley™

Lining the shelves here is every sort of stuffed creature you could imagine. Soft plush versions of everyone's favorites are available for purchase, including Crookshanks the cat, Hedwig the owl, and Buckbeak the hippogriff.

4 **Quality Quidditch™ Supplies**

MAP T1 ■ Diagon Alley™

This is the place to find everything you need for a game of Quidditch, whether that's a bludger, a quaffle, a snitch, or the appropriate robes. They're well stocked on brooms, too – be sure to pick up your Nimbus 2001.

5 **Wiseacre's Wizarding Equipment**

MAP T1 ■ Diagon Alley™

This celestial-inspired shop, a star-filled sky painted upon the ceiling, is stocked with crystal balls, telescopes, binoculars, compasses, and time turners. If it's made of glass or brass, you're likely to find it here.

6 **Ollivanders™**

This well-stocked wand shop, where the wand chooses the wizard, has a branch in both Hogsmeade and Diagon Alley™ *(see p35)*.

7 **Madam Malkin's Robes for All Occasions**

MAP T1 ■ Diagon Alley™

You can pick up your Hogwarts school uniform ties, scarves, and cardigans, a new wizard hat, and other goodies bearing the logos of Hogwarts' four houses (Gryffindor, Ravenclaw, Hufflepuff and Slytherin).

Treats and sweets at Honeydukes™

8 **Honeydukes™**

MAP T1 ■ Hogsmeade™

This confectionery shop is everything you imagined, its shelves stacked top to bottom with brightly colored sweets and treats. Take your pick from pepper imps, Bertie Bots Every Flavor Beans, treacle fudge, acid pops, cauldron cakes, and more – and don't forget the chocolate frogs.

9 **Filch's Emporium™ of Confiscated Goods**

MAP T1 ■ Hogsmeade™

Most confiscated items are not for sale, but you'll also find here an array of Quidditch clothing and accessories, chess sets, magical creatures, and souvenirs galore.

10 **Dervish and Banges™**

MAP T1 ■ Hogsmeade™

Stop here for magical items such as Sneakoscopes, Spectrespecs, Omnioculars, and *The Monster Book of Monsters*. Also for sale is Hogwarts uniforms and clothing, including robes, T-shirts, and sweatshirts.

See map on p102

Bars, Clubs, and Entertainment

① Lucky Leprechaun
MAP T4 ▪ 7032 International Dr ▪ 407-352-7031

There's karaoke every night at this lively and popular Irish-themed bar, with a great selection of Irish beers.

② The groove™
MAP T1 ▪ CityWalk™ ▪ 407-224-3663 ▪ Over-21s only ▪ Adm

This powerhouse dance club (see p71) has high-energy DJs, as well as several quiet chill-out lounges.

③ Jimmy Buffet's Margaritaville
MAP T1 ▪ CityWalk™ ▪ 407-224-2155

A mecca for Parrot Heads or anyone who wants to have a good time in a tropical setting. Great drinks, food, and live entertainment most evenings.

④ Howl at the Moon
MAP T4 ▪ 8815 International Dr ▪ 407-354-5999 ▪ Adm varies

Rock 'n' roll dueling pianos and signature drinks make this high-energy nightclub a fun adult getaway.

⑤ Bob Marley – A Tribute to Freedom
MAP T1 ▪ CityWalk™ ▪ 407-224-2690 ▪ Over-21s only after 10pm ▪ Occasional adm

Live outdoor reggae music is the big draw here – the bands are usually excellent.

The sign for the Bob Marley venue

⑥ Cuba Libre Rum Bar
MAP T4 ▪ 9101 International Dr ▪ 407-226-1600

DJs spin lively Latin tunes, encouraging dancers to take to the floor, where the salsa, merengue, and bachata reign late at night.

Vintage decor at Cuba Libre

⑦ ICEBAR
MAP T4 ▪ 8967 International Dr ▪ 407-351-0361 ▪ Over-21s only after 9pm

This bar is made completely of ice – warm down coats are provided at the entrance. Time inside this small venue is limited, but there's a lounge outside to party the night away.

⑧ Mango's Tropical Cafe
This high-energy club (see p73) boasts a fabulous dinner show featuring scantily clad dancers – think Vegas meets the tropics and you'll get the idea.

⑨ The Whiskey
MAP E3 ▪ 7563 W. Sand Lake Rd ▪ 407-930-6517

Enjoy rare, popular, and hand picked whiskeys of the world and crafted cocktails here, along with award winning burgers.

⑩ Red Coconut Club
MAP T1 ▪ CityWalk™ ▪ 407-224-3663 ▪ Occasional adm

Hip 1950s retro lounge with three bars on two levels, plus live music and DJs. Choose one of the signature martinis.

Places to Eat

PRICE CATEGORIES
For a three-course meal for one, a glass of house wine, and all unavoidable extra charges including tax.

$ under 30 $$ $30–60 $$$ over 60

1 Norman's
MAP F4 ▪ 4012 Central Florida Pkwy ▪ 407-343-4333 ▪ Pre-arrange vegetarian entrées ▪ $$$
Sample delicious fusion food at this award-winning restaurant (see p77) and enjoy excellent views of the lake and gardens.

2 Texas de Brazil Churrascaria
MAP T1 ▪ 5259 International Dr ▪ 407-355-0355 ▪ $$$
This stylish restaurant boasts a vast buffet laden with accompaniments for the skewers of tasty meats served at your table.

3 Roy's
MAP E3 ▪ 7760 W. Sand Lake Rd ▪ 407-352-4844 ▪ $$
On the menu here are Hawaiian fusion dishes such as sesame-oil-seared mahi-mahi with red Thai curry sauce.

4 Everglades
MAP T3 ▪ 9840 International Dr ▪ 407-996-2385 ▪ $$$
A casual, intimate hotel restaurant with an imaginative chef who produces superb steaks and seafood.

5 Seasons 52
MAP E3 ▪ 7700 W. Sand Lake Rd ▪ 407-354-5212 ▪ No kids' menu ▪ $$
The low-calorie seasonal menu here features mouthwatering dishes such as grilled vegetables and crab-stuffed mushrooms.

6 Oceanaire Seafood Room
MAP T4 ▪ 9101 International Dr ▪ 407-363-4801 ▪ $$$
The best seafood and prime meats are served at this sophisticated restaurant – perfect for an adult evening out. Be sure to try one of the hand-crafted cocktails.

7 Capital Grille
MAP T4 ▪ 9101 International Dr ▪ 407-370-4092 ▪ $$$
Another refined, high-end restaurant, this place specializes in prime grilled meats.

8 Café Tu Tu Tango
MAP T3 ▪ 8625 International Dr ▪ 407-248-2222 ▪ $$
Local artists' work adorns the walls of this Barcelona-inspired eatery. Dishes include black bean soup, shrimp fritters, and quesadillas.

Bright decor at Café Tu Tu Tango

9 Cuba Libre
MAP T4 ▪ 9101 International Dr ▪ 407-226-1600 ▪ $$$
This open-air restaurant boasts a tropical atmosphere, lively Latin music, and a menu of contemporary Cuban cuisine. If that's not enough, there's also late-night salsa dancing.

10 The Palm
MAP T1 ▪ Hard Rock Hotel, 5800 Universal Blvd ▪ 407-503-7256 ▪ $$$
The specialty is high-end steaks, often belly-busters up to a 36-oz (1.2-kg) strip for two – but don't overlook the lobster option.

See map on p102

TOP 10 Kissimmee and Beyond

What used to be a cow town has in the past few decades evolved into an inexpensive hotel enclave for Walt Disney World® tourists. But there's much more to Kissimmee. While US-192 (also called the Irlo Bronson Memorial Highway) is dense with strip malls and hotels, downtown Kissimmee (centered on Broadway and Emmet) was built in the early 1890s and features attractive low-slung buildings, some housing antique and gift shops. The land around the highway is relatively undeveloped, offering access to Florida's rich natural beauty and a terrific variety of outdoor pursuits.

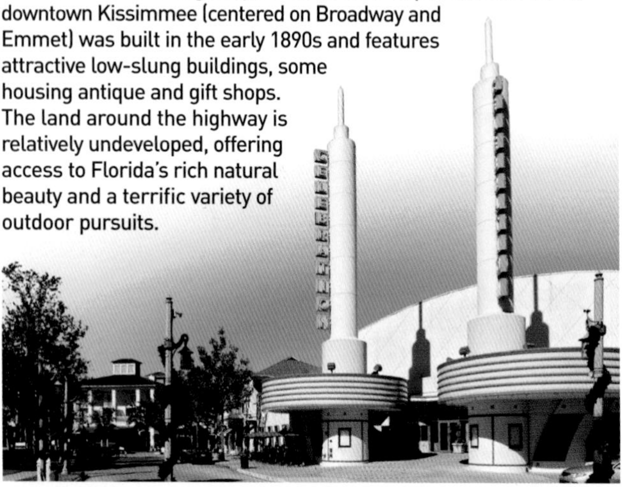

Celebration, Disney's vision of a perfect town

KISSIMMEE AND BEYOND

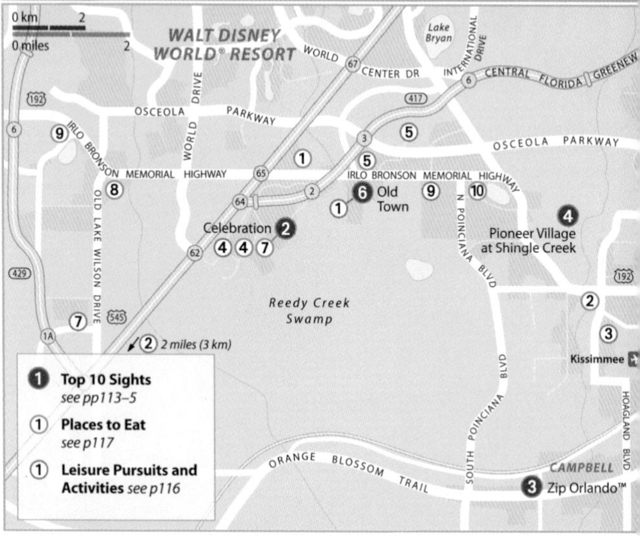

- **1** Top 10 Sights
  see pp113–5
- **1** Places to Eat
  see p117
- **1** Leisure Pursuits and
  Activities see p116

Waterski show at LEGOLAND®

1 LEGOLAND®

Built on part of the former site of Cypress Gardens, Florida's oldest theme park *(see pp36–7)* has captured everyone's imagination. This 150-acre interactive theme park is located just 45 minutes from Orlando and is dedicated to families and children between the ages of 2 and 12. It offers more than 50 rides, shows, attractions, restaurants, and shops, as well as a botanical garden and a water park. There are also life-size LEGO displays along with entertainment options suitable for all ages.

2 Celebration

MAP G2 ▪ Located E. of I-4 at Exit 25; turn right at Celebration Ave and follow the signs

Walt Disney conceived of Epcot® *(see pp16–19)* as a residential community happily road-testing futuristic technologies. After his death, that dream was to resurface years later here. Instead of looking to the future, however, Celebration *(see p83)* salutes the past in an upscale cliché of small-town USA, with some good restaurants. This is not an attraction, but it is quite a sight.

3 Zip Orlando™

MAP H3 ▪ 4509 S. Orange Blossom Trail ▪ 407-808-4947 ▪ Open 9am–6pm Mon–Sat, 12:30–6pm Sun ▪ Adm

Zip on a 950-ft (290-m) line over deer, raccoons, and alligators. Various tours are available *(see p53)*, including guided ATV trips, and moonlit zip-line excursions.

4 Pioneer Village at Shingle Creek

MAP G3 ▪ 2491 Babb Rd ▪ 407-396-8644 ▪ Open 10am–4pm daily ▪ Adm

This outdoor museum offers a glimpse of Kissimmee life pre-Disney. The focal point is a pair of late 1800s Cracker-style cypress wood buildings, complete with cooling "possum trot" breezeway. One re-creates a simple home, the other a general store, selling local history books, crafts, and guides for the nature preserve across the street.

Exhibits at Pioneer Village

5 Merritt Island

Occupying a vast area, this wildlife reserve *(see pp38–9)* is home to endangered species in Florida. Manatees glide in these waters and numerous bird species migrate through these marshlands throughout the year. Explore the area by boat or on foot.

6 Old Town

MAP G2 ▪ 5770 W. Irlo Bronson Memorial Hwy ▪ Open 10am–11pm daily

Essentially, this is a tourist-oriented shopping mall, which is filled with around 75 stores covering the usual array of gifts, novelty items, and souvenirs – kitsch or otherwise. What sets Old Town apart from other gift-shop strips are the numerous entertainment options: a cheerful 18-ride amusement park, Laser Tag, a Haunted House, carousel, live music performances, and a vintage car show that happens every Friday and Saturday night. It's very much about family fun, and there's no charge for admission, although the carnival rides are priced separately. On a warm Florida night, the feeling is one of strolling the bustling midway of a state fair.

Old Town vintage car show

7 Kennedy Space Center Visitor Complex

The sheer size of this complex *(see pp40–43)* makes it a marvel, as it has numerous attractions for all space enthusiasts. There are rockets, historic spacecrafts, and more. Visitors can also opt for shows at the IMAX theaters and learn about modern-day space heroes and explore the world's largest store dedicated to space memorabilia and NASA gear. Dine at one of the themed places for an out-of-the-world experience. Guided bus tours around the spaceport are also available.

8 Forever Florida – Florida Eco-Safaris

MAP B3 ▪ 4755 N. Kenansville Rd, St Cloud ▪ 407-957-9794 ▪ Eco-Safaris on Safari Coaches at 10am and 1pm daily ▪ www.foreverflorida.com

Go back in time to Old Florida on this working cattle ranch and nature preserve. The Forever Florida experience is based on the heritage of the Florida Cracker Cowboy. Take a tour on horseback, fly above the trees on a zip line, or explore nature on an elevated coach. In the evening enjoy a meal at the Cypress Restaurant.

Bird's-eye view, Forever Florida

Splash pad at Lakefront Park

9 Lakefront Park

MAP H6 ■ 1104 Lakefront Blvd, St Cloud

This park (see p57) offers a range of amenities, such as pavilions, picnic areas, and playgrounds, and hosts many community events and periodic concerts. There are several miles of pathways for walkers, joggers, skaters, and cyclists, including a sidewalk by Lake Tohopekaliga, which is popular with birdwatchers. It also has a superb white sand beach, a fishing pier, and an impressive marina. The park has easy access to Kissimmee's historic district, and is close to Chisholm Park and Peghorn Nature Park.

10 Silver Spurs Rodeo

MAP H5 ■ Osceola Heritage Park, 1875 Silver Spur Ln ■ 321-697-3495 ■ www.silverspursrodeo.com

The largest rodeo east of the Mississippi attracts all the top professional cowboys and is held several times a year. The Silver Spurs Rodeo dates back to 1944 and was from 1950 held in a specially constructed open-air arena, until it was replaced by the state-of-the-art, climate-controlled Silver Spurs Arena in 2002. The arena is also used for concerts and sports events, but will always be chiefly associated with the excitement of the rodeo.

A DAY IN KISSIMMEE

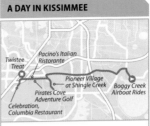

MORNING

There are countless breakfast buffets and restaurants in the area, all offering mounds of food, from fresh fruit to oatmeal, pancakes, and omelets. Find the one closest to you and start the day there. As mornings tend to be cooler and a bit less insect-ridden than afternoons, follow your meal with a self-guided tour of swamp life at Boggy Creek Airboat Rides (see p116). Explore the water-ways, then take a walk along the pathways and enjoy the silence broken only by bird calls. For lunch, head to the quaint Disney-designed town of Celebration, and pop into Columbia Restaurant (see p117) for a sumptuous meal of authentic Cuban cuisine.

AFTERNOON

From Celebration, it's a 6-mile (9.5-km) drive to Pioneer Village at Shingle Creek (see p113). Visit the restored dwellings of the earliest settlers in Osceola County on a self-guided tour, to see the life of Native American tribes. The variety of structures includes a cracker house, blacksmith shop, family homes and a citrus packing house.

EVENING

For dinner, head to Pacino's Italian Ristorante (see p117) for home-style Italian favorites. Afterward, take a short drive to Pirates Cove Adventure Golf (see p116) for a round or two, then head to Twistee Treat in Celebration (2905 W. Parkway Blvd; open 11:30am–10:30pm) for an ice cream to finish your day.

See map on p112 ←

Leisure Pursuits and Activities

 Pirates Cove Adventure Golf

MAP G3 ■ 2845 Florida Plaza Blvd ■ 407-396-7484 ■ Adm

A swashbuckling, tropically landscaped pirate theme has players putt their way through caves and past waterfalls in search of treasure.

2 Bob's Balloon Rides

8293 Championsgate Blvd ■ 407-466-6380 ■ Adm ■ www.bobsballoons.com

Hover high in the sky, taking in the varied landscape – from the lakes and wildlife to the skylines of Central Florida's cities and theme parks.

3 Warbird Adventures

MAP H3 ■ 233 N. Hoagland Blvd ■ 407-870-7366

Take flight in a vintage North American T-6 Texan or a Bell 47 helicopter. You'll even get the chance to take the controls and have the whole experience recorded on DVD.

4 Celebration Golf Club

MAP G2 ■ 701 Golf Park Dr, Celebration ■ 407-566-4653 ■ Adm

Play a challenging round of 18 holes on a course lined by beautiful natural pine forest, set amid the wetlands.

5 Falcon's Fire Golf Club

MAP G3 ■ 3200 Seralago Blvd ■ 407-239-5445 ■ Adm ■ www.falconsfire.com

This immaculately groomed public golf course is said to be one of the best in Florida.

6 Osceola Arts

MAP H5 ■ 2411 E. Irlo Bronson Memorial Hwy ■ 407-846-6257 ■ Adm

Here *(see p49)*, culture mavens will find anything from theater to music events and exhibitions.

7 Orlando Tree Trek Adventure Park

MAP H1 ■ 7625 Sinclair Rd ■ 407-390-9999 ■ Adm

Experience an unusual workout at this aerial adventure course for all ages. Zip lines, climbing nets, and Tarzan swings challenge mind and body.

8 Boggy Creek Airboat Rides

MAP G5 ■ 3702 Big Bass Rd ■ 407-344-9550 ■ Adm

These 18-passenger flat-bottomed skiffs make regular daytime wildlife trips and special one-hour night tours.

9 Museum of Military History

MAP G5 ■ 5210 W. Irlo Bronson Memorial Hwy ■ 407-507-3894 ■ Adm

Interactive exhibits highlight the American military experience from the Civil War through current conflicts.

10 Wild Florida

Lake Cypress Rd, Kennansville ■ 407-957-3135 ■ Adm ■ www.wildfloridaairboats.com

This tour company combines airboat rides through swamps in search of gators and spoonbills, with a wildlife park and cattle ranch.

Wild Florida swamp ride

Places to Eat

PRICE CATEGORIES
For a three-course meal for one with a glass of house wine, and all unavoidable extra charges including tax.

$ under $30 ■ $$ $30–60 ■ $$$ over $60

1 Charley's Steak House
MAP G2 ■ 2901 Parkway Blvd ■ 407-239-1270 ■ Closed lunch ■ $$$

Charley's uses an Indian cooking method, yielding steaks that are charred outside, juicy inside.

Tarantino's Italian Restaurant

2 Tarantino's Italian Restaurant
MAP H3 ■ 4150 W. Vine St ■ 407-870-2622 ■ Closed lunch ■ $$

This delightful Italian venue wins praise for its charming ambience and well-prepared Italian classics.

3 Savion's Place
MAP H4 ■ 16 E. Dakin Ave ■ 407-572-8719 ■ $$

With a casual setting, this eatery offers patrons New American cuisine or dishes with an island flavor.

4 Columbia Restaurant, Celebration
MAP G2 ■ 649 Front St ■ 407-566-1505 ■ $$$

Come here for a taste of old Havana. Indulge in crab-stuffed pompano or enjoy the exquisite calamari.

5 Pacino's Italian Ristorante
MAP G2 ■ 5795 W. Irlo Bronson Memorial Hwy ■ 407-396-8022 ■ $$

Sicilian specialties here include hand-cut steaks, veal chops, and great pizza and pasta.

6 Puerto Rico Cafe
MAP H4 ■ 507 W. Vine St ■ 407-847-6399 ■ $$

It's a bit of a dive, but don't let that put you off trying the delicious *mojo*-enhanced steaks and seafood.

7 Celebration Town Tavern
MAP G2 ■ 721 Front St ■ 407-566-2526 ■ $$

A quiet neighborhood gathering spot, which serves great seafood and burgers. It is family-friendly but also offers happy hours for grown ups. Football games are shown on the big-screen TV.

8 Black Angus Restaurant
MAP G1 ■ 7516 W. Irlo Bronson Memorial Hwy ■ 407-390-4548 ■ $$

Melt-in-your-mouth steaks are the focus of this award-winning family eatery, but ribs and fried chicken are also popular. There's a great breakfast buffet too.

9 Giordano's Italian Restaurant
MAP G2 ■ 7866 W. Irlo Bronson Memorial Hwy ■ 407-397-0044 ■ $$

A casual Italian restaurant, with traditional red-check tablecloths and a menu packed with familiar favorites. This is a great place to bring kids.

10 Taste of the Punjab
MAP G3 ■ 4980 W. Irlo Bronson Memorial Hwy ■ 407-507-3900 ■ $$

A perfect place for an authentic and reasonably priced Indian buffet at either lunch or dinner. Vegetarians are well catered to, with plenty of non-meat dishes on offer.

See map on p112

TOP 10 Downtown Orlando

Orlando is not just about Walt Disney and theme parks. Long a hub of the banking and citrus-growing industries, Downtown Orlando is also a historic district, and a cultural and natural retreat. It contains several of the city's leading museums, as well as its best-known park, a green oasis surrounding Lake Eola, which boasts dramatic skyline vistas. By day Downtown is a relaxed southern enclave, but by night it transforms into a throbbing club scene. Orange Avenue is the main street, where herds of party people, gay and straight, migrate from club to club in search of cheap drinks and hot DJs – and there are plenty of both.

Canna at Harry P. Leu Gardens

DOWNTOWN ORLANDO

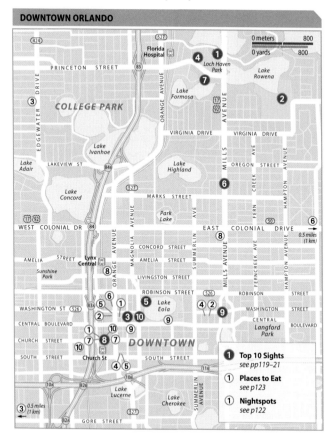

- **1** Top 10 Sights
  see pp119–21
- **1** Places to Eat
  see p123
- **1** Nightspots
  see p122

Exhibition space at the Orlando Museum of Art (OMA)

1 Orlando Museum of Art (OMA)

MAP M3 ■ 2416 N. Mills Ave ■ 407-896-4231 ■ Open 10am–4pm Tue–Fri, noon–4pm Sat–Sun ■ Adm ■ www.omart.org

The focus of exhibitions in this big, bright museum is American art from the 19th century onward, art from the ancient Americas and Africa, and blockbuster traveling shows. On the first Thursday evening of every month, you can enjoy music, food, and the work of local artists at an inventively themed get-together.

2 Harry P. Leu Gardens

MAP M4 ■ 1920 N. Forest Ave ■ 407-246-2620 ■ Open 9am–5pm daily ■ Adm ■ www.leugardens.org

Well-tended pathways weave through this elegant 50-acre park. Earthy scents waft from a herb garden, while another contains plants that attract butterflies. Depending on the season, visitors might catch roses in bloom (in Florida's largest rose garden) or camellias. Guides conduct tours of the early 20th-century Leu House.

3 American Ghost Adventures

MAP P3 ■ Depart from Orange County Regional History Center ■ 407-256-6225 ■ Open 8pm daily ■ Adm

A guide leads walking tours through Downtown Orlando, telling tales of the scandals of the city, unsolved mysteries, and hauntings dating back to 1886. The two-hour walk circles back to its starting point, the Orange County Regional History Center, where participants can carry out their own amateur ghost hunt with the help of handheld "ghost detectors".

Exhibit at Orlando Science Center

4 Orlando Science Center

MAP M3 ■ 777 E. Princeton St ■ 407-514-2000 ■ Open 10am–5pm, closed Wed ■ Adm ■ www.osc.org

The workings of the natural world, from the infinitesimal to the over-whelming, are on display here. Big interactive fun awaits at the Body Zone, where a huge mouth introduces an exhibit about the digestive system. The vast CineDome shows movies about such topics as ancient Egyptian treasures and ocean life, and on weekend evenings, stargazers can pick out the planets through a telescope.

Skyline view, Lake Eola Park

5 Lake Eola Park
MAP P3

A pedestrian-only path encircles Lake Eola, offering a pleasing view of Downtown's skyline. Those willing to exert their leg muscles can rent swan-shaped paddle boats and take to the water *(see p54)*. Real swans drift along in the lake's shallow water and will venture onto dry land if offered a handful of food. Concerts are performed at the Walt Disney Amphitheater, which has surprisingly good acoustics. The landmark illuminated fountain in the middle of the lake *(see p84)* produces a light show of changing colors.

6 The Vietnamese District
MAP N3 ▪ Mills Ave between Virginia Ave and Colonial Dr

This area, also known as the ViMi district (for Virginia and Mills), is a less obvious ethnic enclave than, say, New York's Chinatown. Nevertheless, it is still lined with Vietnamese restaurants and shops, as well as businesses representing other Asian countries, too.

7 Mennello Museum of American Art
MAP M3 ▪ 900 E. Princeton St ▪ 407-246-4278 ▪ Open 10:30am–4:30pm Tue–Sat, noon–4:30pm Sun ▪ Adm ▪ www.mennellomuseum.com

Half of the Mennello is devoted to the work of Florida folk artist Earl Cunningham (1893–1977), who created vibrant, whimsical pastoral paintings glowing with orange skies and yellow rivers. The other half houses traveling exhibits of folk art. The lakeside grounds contain a scattering of quirky sculptures.

8 Church Street
MAP P3 ▪ Between Orange Ave and I-4

The Amway Center has brought life and activity back to Church Street. The influx of restaurants, the renowned theater company Mad Cow Theatre, and the SunRail station have made it even more popular. The Amway Center attracts big-name touring acts, and the stretch of Church Street that lies between Orange Avenue and I-4 has lots of retail stores, restaurants, and bars, keeping visitors amused for hours. The area's original anchor is Church Street Station, a three-level

Restaurant on Church Street

complex constructed around the historic building that was the city's original train station. The complex holds a variety of bars, restaurants, and shops, and it is easy to zigzag between watering holes.

9 Thornton Park
MAP P3

A stylish urban district just east of Lake Eola, including parts of Washington Street, Summerlin Avenue, and Central Boulevard, Thornton Park boasts a number of popular restaurants and eateries (among them Dexter's and Eola Wine Company). Its cobblestone streets are also lined with a number of locally owned shops and boutiques. While a hip neighborhood, its craftsman-style bungalows are one of the area's trademarks.

Orange County Regional History Center

10 Orange County Regional History Center
MAP P3 ▪ 65 E. Central Blvd ▪ 407-836-8500 ▪ Open 10am–5pm Mon–Sat (from noon Sun) ▪ Adm ▪ www.thehistorycenter.org

From the informative to the kitsch, the History Center highlights the formative periods and industries of Central Florida. Dioramas show scenes of early Native Americans, and there's a re-created Florida Cracker house. A display called The Day We Changed chronicles the impact of the arrival of the Disney theme parks. The sinkhole diorama is intriguing, and elements such as the stuffed alligators and pink flamingos betray a sense of fun.

A DAY DOWNTOWN

▶ MORNING

Begin with a hearty American breakfast at the **White Wolf Cafe** (1829 N. Orange Ave) before visiting Loch Haven Park, where the **Orlando Science Center** (see p119), the **Mennello Museum of American Art** (see p120), and the **Orlando Museum of Art (OMA)** (see p119) reside within easy walking distance of each other. The Science Center, with its four floors of interactive fun, is the best bet for kids. Art lovers can easily hit the Mennello and the OMA in the same afternoon but if time is short, the OMA deserves priority. Then wander over to **Citrus** (see p123), for what's repeatedly voted the best power lunch (a business meeting over food) in Orlando.

AFTERNOON

After lunch, head to the **Orange County Regional History Center**, an engaging museum that reveals the region's pre-Disney history. Make a dinner stop in the Vietnamese district, where **Little Saigon** (see p123) serves authentic cuisine, including a delicious hot and spicy rice noodle beef soup.

EVENING

The Downtown club scene starts late, so kick off with an early cocktail at **The Bösendorfer Lounge** (see p122). Fans of live music should head to **The Social** (see p122), where shows start around 10pm. The rooftop **One80 Skytop Lounge** (see p122), is the perfect spot for cocktails and drinks. Enjoy great views of the city from here.

See map on p118 ←

Nightspots

Crowds gather to party at **Wall Street Plaza**

1 Wall Street Plaza
MAP P3 ■ 26 Wall St

A collection of bars, clubs, and eateries – among them Cantina, the Hen House, Hooch, Shine, the Monkey Bar, and Waitiki. Expect a vibrant and loud crowd here.

2 The Beacham
MAP P3 ■ 46 N. Orange Ave ■ 407-648-8363

This historic building houses a state-of-the-art nightclub and live music venue showcasing various genres.

3 Cowboys Orlando
MAP P2 ■ 1108 S. Orange Blossom Trail ■ 407-422-7115 ■ Closed Sun–Wed

This gigantic country music hot spot has four huge bars and nightly dance contests.

4 Bösendorfer Lounge
MAP P3 ■ Grand Bohemian Hotel, 325 S. Orange Ave ■ 407-313-9000

This elegant venue is perfect for sipping stylish cocktails. Lounge singers and pianists perform at the prized Bösendorfer piano (Fri & Sat) (see p68).

5 The Social
MAP P3 ■ 54 N. Orange Ave ■ 407-246-1419

Orlando's best live music club, hosting an incredible variety of acts, from jazz to electronica (see p68).

6 The Courtesy Bar
MAP P3 ■ 114 N. Orange Ave ■ 407-450-2041

A trendy speakeasy bar serving beer, cocktails, absinthe, and wine. Arrive early to secure a seat, as it gets busy.

7 Church Street

A two-block strip of bars, clubs, and restaurants that draws individuals looking for amusement after a symphony at the Dr. Phillips Center (see p48) or a game at the Amway Center (see p120).

8 Ace Café Orlando
MAP P3 ■ 100 W. Livingston St ■ 407 996 6686

Enjoy the Orlando version of this London-based motor-diner with live music. It is a perfect place for those who are passionate about bikes, cars and rock 'n roll.

9 Aku Aku Tiki Bar
MAP P3 ■ 431 E. Central Blvd ■ 407-839-0080

Hawaiian and South Seas kitsch from the 1940s and 1950s makes for a unique atmosphere amid the high-tech Downtown clubs. The bowl-sized rum punches are highly potent.

10 One80 Skytop Lounge
MAP D4 ■ 400 W. Church St ■ 407-913-0180

Located in the Amway Center, this rooftop hotspot offers spectacular city views. There's VIP seating. Reservation recommended.

Places to Eat

1 The Rusty Spoon
MAP P3 ▪ 55 W. Church St
▪ 407-401-8811 ▪ $$

A creative farm-to-table menu contains sections such as leafy greens, handhelds, sustenance, and sweet finish. Excellent service.

2 Graffiti Junction American Burger Bar
MAP P2 ▪ 700 E. Washington St
▪ 407-426-9502 ▪ $$

A graffiti-covered exterior belies the great, high-energy burger joint within. Sunday afternoon karaoke.

3 K Restaurant and Wine Bar
MAP M2 ▪ 1710 Edgewater Dr ▪ 407-872-2332 ▪ Closed Sun ▪ $$$

Downtown's best dining experience offers an adventurous menu of Asian, French, and Italian influences.

4 Dexter's of Thornton Park
MAP P3 ▪ 808 E. Washington St
▪ 407-648-2777 ▪ $$

A favorite after-work hangout, Dexter's offers exotic sandwiches and hearty salads and entrées.

5 The Boheme
MAP P3 ▪ 325 S. Orange Ave
▪ 407-581-4700 ▪ $$$

This outstanding restaurant (see p77), with its sensual paintings and dark woods, serves game, steaks, and seafood to an upscale clientele.

Fabulous art at The Boheme

PRICE CATEGORIES
For a three-course meal for one with a glass of house wine, and all unavoidable extra charges including tax.

$ under $30 $$ $30–60 $$$ over $60

6 Baja Burrito Kitchen
MAP N4 ▪ 2716 E. Colonial Dr
▪ 407-895-6112 ▪ $

This laid-back counter-service eatery (see p78) provides delicious Californian and Mexican cuisine.

7 Ceviche Tapas Bar & Restaurant
MAP P2 ▪ 125 W. Church St
▪ 321-281-8140 ▪ Closed lunch
▪ $$

Huge, noisy, and loads of fun, this restaurant offers an enormous menu, a tapas bar, and a large lounge with live flamenco music.

8 Little Saigon
MAP N3 ▪ 1106 E. Colonial Dr
▪ 407-423-8539 ▪ $$

Set in the city's thriving Vietnamese area, this place serves huge bowls of pho (a fragrant, and spicy soup brimming with meat, seafood, and noodles).

9 Harp & Celt
MAP P3 ▪ 25 S. Magnolia Ave
▪ 407-481-2928 ▪ $$

Traditional Irish pub fare is on offer, along with eclectic daily specials, and drinks are served at a turn-of-the-century bar. The outdoor patio opens when the weather is good.

10 Kres Chophouse
MAP P2 ▪ 17 W. Church St
▪ Closed Sun & lunch Sat ▪ 407-447-7950 ▪ $$$

An upscale restaurant set in a landmark 1930s building, Kres prides itself on its creative, modern approach. Feast on locally sourced dishes, such as melt-in-your-mouth filet Wellington, or red grouper from the Florida Keys.

See map on p118

TOP 10 Winter Park, Maitland, and Eatonville

True to its name, Winter Park was chartered in 1887 as a winter resort for wealthy – and cold – northerners. Now almost completely surrounded by metropolitan Orlando, it still retains the charm and character of a small, wealthy town, with excellent stores and boutiques, bars and restaurants, and a sprinkling of interesting museums. The towns of Maitland and Eatonville, to the north and west, are more residential. They have a number of worthwhile attractions, which can make a pleasant change from south Orlando's bustling, commercialized theme parks.

Audubon National Center for Birds of Prey

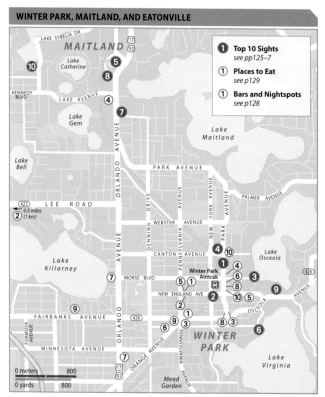

WINTER PARK, MAITLAND, AND EATONVILLE

① **Top 10 Sights**
see pp125–7

① **Places to Eat**
see p129

① **Bars and Nightspots**
see p128

1 Park Avenue
MAP L4

The stretch of Park Avenue between Fairbanks and Webster avenues is a thriving slice of urban living. This is the kind of manageable, old-style downtown that is usually erased in the rush to suburbanize. There's bucolic Central Park to explore and the short buildings contain fashionable shops or eateries that will keep you occupied all day long.

2 Winter Park Farmers' Market
MAP L4 ■ 721 W. New England Ave ■ 407-599-3397 ■ Open 7am–1pm Sat

Some farmers' markets are serious business, packed with old trucks and farmers selling mountains of vegetables just pulled from the earth. The Winter Park Farmers' Market is altogether a different affair. Locals come here to mingle, buy potted flowers, preserves, and herbs, and indulge in fresh croissants, muffins, and breads. There are vegetables here, too, but this is more of a coffee and brunch gathering.

3 Winter Park Scenic Boat Tour
MAP L4 ■ Morse Blvd at Lake Osceola ■ 407-644-4056 ■ Tours depart on the hour 10am–4pm daily ■ Adm

The wealthiest sections of Winter Park were built around a series of lakes and along winding canals. This boat tour *(see p53)* has been running since 1938, and is part nature trip and part local history lesson. It cruises lazily past Winter Park landmarks and mansions encountering wildlife, while the skipper tells stories about the legendary society crowd.

Winter Park Scenic Boat Tour

The restored Tiffany Chapel

4 Charles Hosmer Morse Museum of American Art
MAP L4 ■ 445 N. Park Ave ■ 407-645-5311 ■ Open 9:30am–4pm Tue–Sat (to 8pm Fri Nov–Apr), 1–4pm Sun ■ Adm ■ www.morsemuseum.org

This museum contains the world's largest collection of glass windows and objects by artist Louis Comfort Tiffany. Other highlights include ceramics and collections of late 19th- and early 20th-century paintings, graphics, and decorative arts.

5 Lake Lily Park
MAP K3 ■ 701 Lake Lily Dr, Maitland ■ 407-539-6200

This park is made up of 5 acres of lush landscaping around Lake Lily, offering visitors plenty of secluded, shady areas for picnics. There's also a quiet board-walk that winds beside the lake, jogging trails, and the restored historic Waterhouse Residence Museum.

Paintings on display at the Cornell Fine Arts Museum

⑥ Cornell Fine Arts Museum

MAP L4 ■ 1000 Holt Ave ■ 407-646-2526 ■ Open 10am–4pm Tue–Fri, noon–5pm Sat–Sun ■ www.rollins.edu/cfam

The art collection at this museum, located on the scenic Rollins College Campus, is one of the oldest in the state. The range of European and American art – dating from the Renaissance to the 20th century – is impeccably presented and of an unusually high quality for a small college art museum.

⑦ Enzian Theater

MAP K3 ■ 1300 S. Orlando Ave ■ 407-629-1088 ■ Open evenings daily & weekend afternoons ■ Adm ■ www.enzian.org

The art of film has a different flavor at the Enzian. This not-for-profit 250-seat theater doesn't just show American independent and foreign films, but also offers a full menu with beer, wine, and table service. Relax with dinner or snacks and enjoy films with all the comforts of your own living room (with the addition of a 33-ft (10-m) wide screen). The Enzian is also responsible for the 10-day Florida Film Festival (see p86) and puts on smaller, niche festivals throughout the year.

⑧ Historic Waterhouse Residence and Carpentry Shop Museum

MAP K3 ■ 820 Lake Lily Dr ■ 407-644-2451 ■ Open noon–4pm Thu–Sun ■ Adm ■ artandhistory.org/waterhouse-museum

William H. Waterhouse was a carpenter who came to Central Florida in the early 1880s and built this lovely home overlooking Lake Lily. Pristinely restored and maintained by the Maitland Historical Society, the home, Waterhouse's carpentry shop, and the property's remarkable collection of handcrafted furniture offer a glimpse into Maitland's past. Woodworking buffs will be wowed by Waterhouse's extensive use of heart of pine, a wood rarely seen today. Tours lasting about 40 minutes are offered. The Waterhouse facilities complement the Maitland Historical Museum, Maitland Art Center, and Telephone Museum (see p47), all just a few blocks away and also run by the Maitland Historical Society.

Tables and chairs at Enzian Theater

9 Albin Polasek Museum and Sculpture Gardens

MAP L4 ■ 633 Osceola Ave ■ 407-647-6294 ■ Open 10am–4pm Tue–Sat, 1–4pm Sun ■ Adm ■ www.polasek.org

Sculptor Albin Polasek moved here to retire from his job, but he kept on producing his figurative works until his death in 1965. Now listed on the National Register of Historic Places, the museum and its sculpture gardens contain works spanning Polasek's entire career.

Sculpture in the gardens of the Albin Polasek Museum

10 Audubon Center for Birds of Prey

MAP K3 ■ 1101 Audubon Way ■ 407 644-0190 ■ Open 10am–4pm Tue–Sun ■ Adm ■ www.audubonofflorida.org

Think of this place as a halfway house for some of Florida's most impressive birds. It was created by the Florida Audubon Society to rescue, rehabilitate, and release wounded raptors (birds of prey). Those that wouldn't survive being released into the wild are kept here, living a pampered existence in a lovely lakeside location, while helping to educate visitors about wildlife issues and conservation. Visitors aren't allowed to observe the rehabilitation process itself, but permanent residents on view usually include vultures, bald eagles, screech owls, hawks, ospreys, and more.

A DAY IN WINTER PARK

- Enzian Theater
- Charles Hosmer Morse Museum of American Art
- Briarpatch Restaurant
- Winter Park Scenic Boat Tour
- Park Avenue
- Hillstone
- Luma on Park
- Cornell Fine Arts Museum

▶ MORNING

Begin with a hearty breakfast at the **Briarpatch Restaurant** *(252 N. Park Ave; 407-628-8651).* You'll probably have to wait a bit, especially on weekends, so grab a newspaper. Afterward, take time to wander the north end of **Park Avenue** *(see p125),* where a multitude of charming one-off boutiques cater to upscale shopping tastes. At Canton Avenue pop in to the **Charles Hosmer Morse Museum of American Art** *(see p125);* its outstanding collection of Tiffany glass is a must-see. Follow this with a relaxing trip on the **Winter Park Scenic Boat Tour** *(see p125),* which departs from a dock on Morse Boulevard, just a 15-minute walk away. On your return, lunch options are plentiful, but if the weather is good, make sure you grab one of the sidewalk tables at **Luma on Park** *(see p129)* for some good food and people-watching.

AFTERNOON

After lunch, continue south on Park Avenue to Rollins College, home of the excellent **Cornell Fine Arts Museum** and spend the rest of the afternoon enjoying this small but excellent collection.

EVENING

It's a 10-minute car ride north to Maitland's **Enzian Theater**, where you can settle in to enjoy the latest in independent films with a bottle of wine and a cheese plate. End the day with a lakeside meal at **Hillstone** *(see p129),* just a few minutes south by car.

See map on p124

Bars and Nightspots

Outdoor seating at Hannibal's on the Square

1 **Hannibal's on the Square**
MAP L4 ▪ 511 W. New England Ave ▪ 407-629-4865
Part café, part casual upscale bar, Hannibal's shares seating space with a tremendous French restaurant.

2 **Dexter's of Winter Park**
MAP L4 ▪ 558 W. New England Ave ▪ 407-629-1150
Home to a serious collection of wines, this branch of Dexter's is more upscale than its Downtown location. Featured bands play classic rock.

3 **Fiddler's Green**
MAP L4 ▪ 544 W. Fairbanks Ave ▪ 407-645-2050 ▪ $$
This energetic Irish pub has darts, music, and a selection of draft beers and stouts. The food is good too. It stays open until 2am most nights.

4 **Copper Rocket Pub**
MAP K3 ▪ 106 Lake Ave ▪ 407-645-0069
With its small stage hosting anything from jazz jams to psychedelia, this is the only real music bar in the area. Microbrews fuel the young audience.

5 **Hamilton's Kitchen**
MAP L4 ▪ Alfond Inn, 300 E. New England Ave ▪ 407-998-8090 ▪ $$$
This classy cocktail haven in a chic hotel also boasts a go-to Sunday brunch at the chef-driven restaurant.

6 **The Parkview**
MAP L4 ▪ 136 Park Ave ▪ 407-647-9103
An extensive menu of wines by the glass is on offer at this wine shop and bar. Drinks are complemented by a wide range of snacks and desserts.

7 **Marlow's Tavern**
MAP L3 ▪ 1008 S. Orlando Ave ▪ 407-960-3670 ▪ $$
Black and white photos adorn brick walls of this modern tavern. Fill up on gourmet flatbreads, salads, and burgers, or more substantial fare.

8 **The Wine Room**
MAP L4 ▪ 270 S. Park Ave ▪ 407-696-9463 ▪ $$
Wine is showcased here, with over 156 bottles hand-selected for sampling. There is also a selection of artisan cheeses and a tapas-style menu.

9 **The Porch**
MAP L3 ▪ 643 Orange Ave ▪ 407-571-9101 ▪ Closed Mon ▪ $$
The comprehensive list of cocktails, beers, and wines is accompanied by a menu featuring burgers, wings, and other home-style favorites.

10 **Park Social**
MAP L4 ▪ 358 N. Park Ave ▪ 407-636-7020 ▪ Closed Sun–Tue
Retro cocktail lounge serving craft cocktails and tapas-style plates. A DJ spins tracks on Friday and Saturday nights.

Places to Eat

PRICE CATEGORIES

For a three-course meal for one with a glass of house wine, and all unavoidable extra charges including tax.

$ under 30	$$ $30–60	$$$ over $60

1 Ravenous Pig
MAP L4 ■ 565 W. Fairbanks Ave ■ 321-280-4200 ■ $$$

Local, organic, and Southern food by James Beard-nominated chefs is served alongside a wide choice of drinks at this brewery and kitchen.

2 Christner's Prime Steak & Lobster
MAP C4 ■ 729 Lee Rd ■ 407-645-4443 ■ $$$

At this family-owned restaurant (see p76), locally-sourced ingredients are used, along with imported cold-water lobster and the best cuts of beef.

3 Café de France
MAP L4 ■ 526 S. Park Ave ■ 407-647-1869 ■ No kids' menu ■ $$

Despite the name, this eatery has an international menu served in an upbeat setting. There are no vegetarian dishes available.

4 Prato
MAP L4 ■ 124 W. Park Ave ■ 407-262-0050 ■ Closed lunch Mon & Tue ■ $$$

Enjoy year-round outdoor seating at this restaurant that offers classic Italian cuisine. A wall of tropical plants complements the ambience.

5 Mynt Fine Indian Cuisine
MAP L3 ■ 535 W. New England Ave ■ 407-636-7055 ■ $$

An elegant venue for an authentic Indian feast, inspired by a variety of culinary influences. There are plenty of meat-free dishes too.

6 Winter Park Fish Company
MAP L3 ■ 761 Orange Ave ■ 407-622-6112 ■ Closed Sun ■ $$

This family-owned counter-service eatery serves diners on picnic tables. First pick your fish, then choose how you want it prepared, add a topping, and pick two sides.

7 Hillstone
MAP L3 ■ 215 S. Orlando Ave ■ 407-740-4005 ■ $$

A wood-burning grill dominates this lovely waterfront restaurant where locals come to witness the sunset over the lake. Portions are huge, particularly the salads and desserts. There are also seafood options.

8 Umi
MAP L4 ■ 525 S. Park Ave ■ 407-960-3993 ■ $$

Japanese fusion cuisine with a side of sushi is what you'll find on Umi's creative menu, but with a twist. Plates are served tapas-style, allowing everyone to share the artfully presented dishes.

Sharing plate at Umi

9 Rivers Smokehouse
MAP L3 ■ 1600 W Fairbanks Ave ■ 407-474-8377 ■ $$

The award-winning modern barbecue served here features ribs, brisket, pork, chicken, and homestyle sides. Be sure not to miss the red velvet cake and other decadent desserts.

10 Luma on Park
MAP L4 ■ 290 S. Park Ave ■ 407-599-4111 ■ No kids' menu ■ Closed lunch ■ $$

An award-winning chef, superlative cuisine, a head-spinning wine list, and an ultra-hip environment can be found at Luma on Park, which is why it's always packed with stylish people.

See map on p124

Streetsmart

The colorful scenery of Dr. Seuss at the Seuss Landing
area of Universal's Islands of Adventure™

Getting To and Around Orlando

Arriving by Air

Three airports serve Orlando: **Orlando International Airport**, **Orlando Sanford International Airport**, and **Orlando Executive Airport**.

Orlando International Airport is the city's busiest airport, handling the majority of national and international flights in and out of Orlando. It is located 12 miles (20 km) southeast of the city center and 20 miles (32 km) northeast of the main tourist districts. There are taxis, shuttle services, hotel shuttles, and rental cars located at ground level, below the arrival area, and outside of baggage claim. The cost of a taxi ride to the tourist districts ranges between $38 and $75, depending on your final destination. Public transportation, via the LYNX bus, is available; however, service is limited to two stops located in the city and two stops along International Drive.

Orlando Sanford International Airport is located 23 miles (37 km) northeast of the city center and 48 miles (77 km) from the major tourist districts. Taxis, private shuttles, and rental cars are available for hire, but there is no public transportation.

Orlando Executive Airport is serviced only by private jet and charter plane. It is 3 miles (5 km) from the city.

Arriving by Train

Trains operated by **Amtrak** offer service via stations located in Downtown Orlando, Kissimmee, Winter Park, and Sanford – all of which connect to destinations across the US. The Auto Train (operated by Amtrak) offers round-trip services to and from Lorton, Virginia, arriving in Sanford, Florida, allowing passengers to bring their car while traveling by train. International visitors can buy a USA Rail Pass for 15, 30, or 45 days of unlimited travel.

Arriving by Bus

A national bus service operated by **Greyhound** links many parts of the country to Orlando, with stations located both in the city and in the tourist district of Kissimmee.

Traveling by Train

The **SunRail** commuter train connects stations running from north, Kissimmee through Downtown Orlando, Winter Park, Sanford, and across the St. Johns to DeBary. The service runs on weekdays until 9pm, and sporadically on the weekend.

Traveling by Bus and Trolley

The city's local **LYNX** bus system provides public transportation throughout the entire area, including the city and tourist districts. Bus stations are marked with a paw print, with buses displaying destinations on the front or side. Tickets can be purchased online or at a number of Ace Cash Express locations throughout the area. Exact change is required if paying when boarding the bus.

The **I-Ride Trolley** provides hop-on/hop-off transportation that runs the length of International Drive and Universal Blvd (both on the green line). Trolleys run every 20–30 minutes, operating between the hours of 8:30am and 10pm. Pay as you board the trolley, or go online to buy passes for up to 14 days.

Traveling by Car

The sheer volume of traffic in the main tourist areas of Orlando can pose some challenges for drivers. Traffic is heavy along I-4, US 192, 535, and 536. The busiest times are early in the morning, during the early evening, and late at night. Most visitors arrive by air and rent a car to get around. Rental companies include **Alamo**, **Avis**, **Budget**, and **National**; these businesses are located at the airports, as well as at a small number of larger hotels.

To rent a car in Orlando, you are required to have a valid driver's license and (for international travelers only) a passport, and you must be at least 21 years of age. Additional fees apply if you are between 21 and 24 years of age. Credit cards are the only acceptable form of payment – no debit cards.

Traveling by Taxi

You can hail a taxi in front of most hotels, resorts, at

major attractions, and at the airport. You can call for taxi services such as **Star Taxi, Diamond Cab Company, Ace Metro/ Luxury Cab,** and **Mears Taxi Yellow.** Expect the meter to start at around $3.25 for the first mile, then add a charge of $2 or more per mile after that. A ride to or from the airports can be $38–75 depending on your destination. Lyft and Uber are available in the area.

Traveling by Bicycle

Cycling is a fun alternative to walking around the city, and the area is filled with bike paths. Rentals are available at a number of locations for recreational use, including **West Orange Trail Bikes & Blades.** In the city center, **Juice Bike Share** allows you to reserve a bike online or via your smart-

phone, pick it up at any of the citywide locations (some found north of the city), then simply return it to one of the authorized racks or hub locations.

Traveling on Foot

The city center is easily explored by foot. The theme parks also have walkable areas, but travel between hotels and attractions is best accomplished by a vehicle. Away from the center, Orlando has been ranked as one of the most dangerous cities for pedestrians, due to the wide highways and a lack of sidewalks, crosswalks, and streetlights.

Theme Park Transportation

Disney has a vast transportation system – free for all visitors to

Disney theme parks – that features buses, water taxis, ferries, and a monorail.

The bus system links every on-site hotel, the four major theme parks, water parks, and Disney Springs™. It runs 45 mins prior to park opening until two hours after closing.

Water taxis and ferries operate between select on-site resorts and theme parks, while the monorail – the quickest mode of transportation – links the Magic Kingdom® to a handful of Disney's hotels, Epcot®, and the Ticket & Transportation area.

Universal Orlando Resort™ runs buses between the on-site hotels and theme parks. There is also a water-taxi service between CityWalk®, The Hard Rock Hotel, Royal Pacific Hotel, and Portofino Bay Hotel. Transportation is free for guests.

Practical Information

Passports and Visas

International visitors are required to present a valid e-passport and must register online with the Electronic System for Travel Authorization (**ESTA**) well in advance of travel.

Citizens of the 38 countries participating in the Visa Waiver Program (VWP) – including the UK, South Africa, Italy, New Zealand, Australia, France, and many other European countries – may visit for up to 90 days for business or pleasure without a visa if they have a valid e-passport. Other nationals should apply for a visa from their local US consulate or embassy well in advance of travel. Canadians need only a valid passport for travel to the US.

Passports should be valid for a minimum of six months beyond their date of entry. For the most up-to-date information on requirements for entry into the United States, check the **US Department of State** website.

A number of countries including the **UK**, **Ireland**, **Australia**, **New Zealand**, and **Canada** have consulates in Florida and are able to provide consular assistance to their nationals.

Customs and Immigration

Visitors to the US aged 21 and older may bring in, free of duty, 1 quart (945 ml) of alcohol; 200 cigarettes, 50 cigars, or 3 lb (1.3 kg) of smoking tobacco; and $100 worth of gifts. These limits are offered to visitors spending a minimum of 72 hours in the US who have not claimed them within the preceding six-month period.

It is forbidden to bring into the country any meat products, fruits, or vegetables. International visitors may bring up to $10,000 in US currency without having to declare it to US customs. For additional details on regulations, visit the **U.S. Customs and Border Protection** website.

Travel Safety Advice

Visitors can get up-to-date travel safety information from the **UK Foreign and Commonwealth Office**, the **US Department of State**, and the **Australian Department of Foreign Affairs and Trade**.

Travel Insurance

All travelers are advised to buy insurance against emergency medical and dental care, theft or loss, accidents, and travel delays or cancelations. The US does not have a reciprocal health agreement with other nations, and visitors must be able to pay up front for healthcare costs they incur while traveling.

Rental car companies offer vehicle coverage, but do check before you take out any additional insurance, since you may be covered through your bank, travel, or home policy.

Health

There are no vaccinations required for entry into the US, and there are few serious health hazards. Tap water is drinkable, though bottled water is readily available. Prescription medication should always be carried in hand baggage and kept in the original containers with pharmacy labels, so they pass easily through airport security.

For minor ailments, it is best to go to the local pharmacy or grocery store, where over-the-counter medications are available. Pharmacies are generally open from 8am to 9 or 10pm Monday through Saturday, with shortened hours on Sundays.

A small number of 24-hour pharmacies are also located in the tourist areas. These include a CVS Pharmacy at 7599 Sand Lake Road and a Walgreens at 8959 International Drive.

If you become ill or hurt while in the theme parks, first-aid stations can provide assistance. There are also house-call services offered through **Doctors on Call** and **The Medical Concierge**, where doctors provide minor medical services at your hotel room – convenient if you are without a car. Payment is expected at the time of service.

For more serious medical ailments, there are several walk-in care clinics where no appointment is necessary and two major hospitals. Walk-in clinics include **Lake Buena Vista Centra Care** and **Dr. Phillips**

Centra Care. The city's major hospitals are the **Florida Hospital** and the **Orlando Regional Medical Center**.

Personal Security

Orlando is a relatively safe city, although its crime rate is equivalent to that of other large US cities. The usual advice given to anyone traveling in a large city, or a bustling tourist area, applies.

Leave all of your valuables, including your passport, in the hotel safe. Most hotel rooms have a small safe in the closet or dresser drawer. Carry as little cash as possible, and hide what you do have in a money belt under your clothing. Carry wallets in front pockets, and ensure that

bags are strapped across your front. Be alert to pickpockets, particularly in crowded amusement parks. At night, avoid badly lit areas (especially Downtown's westside, south of Colonial Drive).

Thieves often work in pairs, with one distracting you as the other is stealing your items, so be alert if someone attempts to distract you.

Lockers are located at most of the major attractions and are a safe place to store your valuables while exploring the theme parks. Fingerprint and electronic codes ensure only you will be able to gain access. Some charge a small fee, but others are free. Expect to have your bags inspected as you enter any of the major attractions

in the area. While the security checkpoint adds to the time waiting in line to enter the parks, it helps ensure no one is bringing something they shouldn't be.

Report all lost or stolen items to the police, and make sure you get a copy of the police report for your insurance claim at home. If your passport goes missing, you must contact the embassy of your home country immediately. The US Department of State website has contact information for all foreign embassies in the US.

Emergency Services

For **ambulance, police, and fire** services, dial the countrywide emergency number 911.

DIRECTORY

PASSPORTS AND VISAS

Australia
☎ 202-797-3000

Canada
☎ 202-682-1740

ESTA
🌐 esta.cbp.dhs.gov

Ireland
☎ 202-462-3939

New Zealand
☎ 202-328-4800

UK
☎ 202-588-6500

US Department of State
🌐 usvisas.state.gov
🌐 state.gov

CUSTOMS AND IMMIGRATION

U.S. Customs and Border Protection
🌐 cbp.gov

TRAVEL SAFETY ADVICE

Australian Department of Foreign Affairs and Trade
🌐 dfat.gov.au
🌐 smartraveller.gov.au

UK Foreign and Commonwealth Office
🌐 gov.uk/foreign-travel-advice

US Department of State
🌐 travel.state.gov

HEALTH

Doctors on Call
☎ 407-399-3627

Dr. Phillips Centra Care
MAP E3 ■ 8014 Conroy Windermere Rd #104
☎ 407-291-8975

Florida Hospital
MAP C5 ■ 601 E. Rollins St
☎ 407-303-4000
🌐 florida hospital.com

Lake Buena Vista Centra Care
MAP F2 ■ 12500 S. Apopka Vineland Rd
☎ 407 934-2273

The Medical Concierge
☎ 407-648-5252
🌐 themedical concierge.com

Orlando Regional Medical Center
MAP D5 ■ 52 W. Underwood St
☎ 321-841-5111

EMERGENCY SERVICES

Ambulance, Police, and Fire
☎ 911

Travelers With Specific Needs

The Americans with Disabilities Act has ensured that the majority of public establishments in the US (including hotels, restaurants, attractions, and at least some modes of transportation) provide accessible entrances and other facilities for those with specific needs. In addition, most attractions offer assistance in the form of wheelchair rentals, electric scooter rentals, and accessible entrances.

Public buses, along with Disney and Universal buses, have hydraulic lifts and restraining belts for wheelchairs. The Disney monorail and select watercraft traveling between the theme parks and resorts are also equipped for wheelchairs.

Services at the parks include special parking, assisted listening devices, and special park guides that outline all of the services available to disabled guests while at the theme parks. **Medical Travel Inc.** offers wheelchair van rentals, while mobility scooters and medical equipment can be rented from **Walker Medical and Mobility Products** and **Care Medical Equipment**.

Currency and Banking

The US currency is the US dollar, which divides into 100 cents. Paper notes are in denominations of $1, $5, $10, $50, $100, and $500. Coins are in denominations of 1¢, 5¢, 10¢, 25¢, 50¢, and $1.

ATMs are the easiest way to get cash, but be aware that some US ATMs charge a hefty fee for withdrawals made with another bank's card.

Prepaid bank cards offer a safe alternative to carrying cash and can be preloaded prior to your trip and used at ATMs, restaurants, and stores, much like a debit card.

Credit cards are widely accepted, even in smaller shops and restaurants. When using a credit card, the most current exchange rates are automatically applied to your purchases. If your card is lost or stolen, be sure to contact the police and your credit card company.

Telephone and Internet

Orlando International Airport, along with most hotels and restaurants, offers Wi-Fi or high-speed Internet access. While some places offer access free of charge, many hotels charge a fee of at least $9.99 to use the service for a 24-hour period.

The dialing code for the US is 1, and the city code for Orlando is 407. Phone numbers must always be dialed in full (all 10 digits), even when making local calls.

Postal Services

Main branches of the **US Post Office** are usually open 8am–4pm Monday through Friday and 8am–1pm Saturdays, with select branches open extended hours. Stamped letters and postcards may be dropped off at the front desk of most hotels, where the mailman will pick them up. Currently stamps for a first-class letter cost 49 cents.

Television and Radio

Public television is broadcast on WUCF, the area's only public station. Numerous private stations exist, with ABC, NBC, and CBS stations all represented and broadcast via cable and satellite television, alongside hundreds of additional stations. Select stations broadcast in languages other than English.

Local news channel 13 is Orlando's version of CNN. This 24-hour cable news channel is devoted to the city, with the local weather broadcast every 10 minutes.

Newspapers and Magazines

The **Orlando Sentinel** is the area's only major newspaper. It provides local and national news, as well as dining, entertainment, and business news. The Friday edition includes an entertainment calendar. **Orlando Magazine,** a glossy monthly, includes information about dining, entertainment and arts.

The **Orlando Weekly** is a small free publication featuring entertainment and art listings focusing on areas outside the tourist districts.

Opening Hours

Office hours are generally 9am–6pm Monday through Friday. Some businesses, such as shops and malls, are open 10am–9pm Monday through Saturday and 11am–7pm Sunday.

Banks are generally open 8am–4pm on weekdays; some are open Saturdays 9am–noon (and sometimes to 2pm). Attractions and theme parks have their own operating hours that change seasonally – and sometimes weekly or even daily. It is best to check each individual website for the most up-to-date information.

Time Difference

Orlando operates on Eastern Standard Time, which is 5 hours behind Greenwich Mean Time, and 6 hours behind Central European Time. The clock moves ahead 1 hour during daylight saving time, from the last Sunday in March to the last Sunday in November.

Electrical Appliances

The US uses 110–120 volts AC (60 Hertz), compared to the 220–240 volts AC (50 Hertz) of most European countries. If you are traveling from another country, bring a converter, because they are hard to find in the US – most stores only stock converters for traveling outside of the US.

Weather

Expect a tropical climate with moderate winters, a warm spring and fall, and summers that are hot and humid. Temperatures in July and August reach well into the high 90s Fahrenheit (30s Celsius). Afternoon thunderstorms occur daily in summer and August to September is high hurricane season.

Language

English is the official language in the US; however, large Hispanic and Latino communities mean Spanish is spoken in numerous areas throughout Orlando.

Visitor Information

Information about hotels, restaurants, and attractions in Orlando can be found at the websites of **Visit Florida** and **Visit Orlando**. A Visit Orlando visitors center is located on International Drive, where visitors can pick up printed information and maps and ask for advice.

Trips and Tours

The theme parks all offer their own tours *(see p141)*, but if you are eager to see a little more of the city and surrounding area, there are several tour companies to choose from.

Orlando Tours provides airboat tours of the Everglades and trips to Clearwater Beach, St. Augustine, and Miami, among many other destinations.

Grayline Orlando offers a day's tour of the city, including a guided bus tour of the Downtown area, a narrated boat trip in Winter Park, a trip to shopping district Park Avenue, and a tour of the City of Celebration, Walt Disney's vision of a perfect community.

(see p141)

DIRECTORY

TRAVELERS WITH SPECIFIC NEEDS

Care Medical Equipment
C 800-741-2282
W caremedical equipment.com

Medical Travel Inc.
C 866-322-4400
W medicaltravel.org

Walker Medical and Mobility Products
C 888-726-6837
W walkermobility.com

POSTAL SERVICES

US Post Office
10450 Turkey Lake Road
C 407-351-2492
8am–7pm Mon–Fri, 9am–5pm Sat

NEWPAPERS AND MAGAZINES

Orlando Magazine
W orlandomagazine. com

Orlando Sentinel
W orlandosentinel.com

Orlando Weekly
W orlandoweekly.com

VISITOR INFORMATION

Visit Florida
W visitflorida.com
W orlando.com

Visit Orlando
MAP E3 ▪ 8723 International Drive
C 407-363-5872
W visitorlando.com

TRIPS AND TOURS

Grayline Orlando
W graylineorlando.com

Orlando Tours
W orlando-tours.com

Shopping

Orlando offers a unique array of shopping opportunities. Within the main theme parks there are numerous one-of-a-kind specialty shops offering merchandise that cannot be found elsewhere. These include the Diagon Alley™ and Hogsmeade™ shops in Universal Studios Florida™ (see p107) and Universal's Islands of Adventure™ (see pp30–3), **Universal Orlando Resort™, Walt Disney World®** and the boutiques at **Disney Springs™**.

There are also a number of inviting outlet malls filled with designer goods at great prices. **Orlando International Premium Outlets** and **Orlando Vineland Premium Outlets** offer some real bargains.

The best shopping malls include the **Mall at Millenia** and Florida Mall (see p82). Park Avenue, a shopping district in Winter Park, features lots of upscale boutiques and trendy independent shops.

Purchases are subject to a 6 per cent sales tax, barring grocery items and some medications.

Dining

In Orlando you'll find well over 5,000 restaurants and eateries that range from fast food to fine dining, ensuring an array of options to please every taste and budget.

Outside of the parks is a plethora of chain restaurants, most offering a casual atmosphere, moderate pricing, and a familiar menu, while select high-end chains boast menus of prime meats and seafood, crafted cocktails and extensive wine cellars, delivered by stellar chefs and wait staff. There is also a handful of independent options (some reaching into the tourist areas) offering better-than-average menus and a sophisticated setting.

Within the main tourist areas, restaurants can be found in clusters. Good locations include the length of International Drive, the Dr. Phillips area, Universal's CityWalk™, and Disney Springs™.

Inside the theme parks, guests are treated to an array of themed restaurants and culturally diverse cuisine. Character dining is unique to the Orlando area, with a number of restaurants featuring meet-and-greet opportunities coupled with an all-you-can-eat buffet. Dinner shows feature themed entertainment during your meal, a set menu served either family style (large plates set at the table piled high with enough to serve your entire party), or pre-plated.

Reservations, while not required at most restaurants, are highly recommended given the number of people competing for a table – wait times can be two hours or more for a table without a reservation outside the parks, especially between the hours of 6pm and 8:30pm. To make reservations for restaurants away from the resort areas, contact the restaurant directly, or use a booking website like **OpenTable**, which also features guest reviews. **Walt Disney World®** offers an Advanced Reservation system that allows resort guests to book a table 180 days in advance. The park's most popular restaurants are often completely booked out well in advance. At **Universal Orlando Resort™**, reservations can be made at most CityWalk™ and resort restaurants, along with select theme park restaurants. Note, however, that restaurants located inside the theme parks also require theme park admission. Some restaurants and dinner shows require a deposit or, in some cases, full payment in advance.

Special dietary requirements are well catered for in Orlando. Restaurants throughout the parks and resorts now offer gluten-free, and in some instances, kosher options on their regular menu. Disney will happily accommodate those in need of lactose-, sugar- and fat-free options, as well as guests with specific allergies, as long as they are requested at least 24 hours in advance.

Cost-conscious guests can save a bit of money by making lunch their main meal, since prices are often (though not always) slightly lower than during the peak dinner hours. Outside the parks, some restaurants offer "early-bird" specials beginning at 4pm but ending before the usual evening dining hours.

Both Universal and Disney offer dining plans; however, Disney's is restricted to Disney resort guests (offering several plans that give substantial savings), while Universal's is quite simple and the savings more minimal by comparison.

Accommodation

From functional budget options, to lavish resorts and one-off boutique hotels, there are a huge number of hotels to choose from in Orlando (see pp142–7).

The majority of hotels and resorts are located around International Drive and the **Walt Disney World**® Resort; many can be found within the resorts themselves. These hotels offer extra hours in the park, include access to free transportation systems at Disney and Universal (see p132), and ensure close proximity – allowing visitors the luxury of returning to their base for a midday nap or swim. The main drawback to staying on-site is the cost: rates are often about 30 percent more than staying at comparable places outside the resorts.

For those traveling with families, all-suite properties offer extra space, kitchens, and sometimes two TVs. Many modest hotels and motels provide microwaves and small refrigerators. Check whether cots and cribs are available and free of charge, whether kids' menus are offered in the hotel restaurants, and whether the hotel will help with recommended babysitters.

Orlando is filled with condominiums and apartments whose owners rent out their quarters when not in residence. These can provide comfortable living space plus kitchens, but there is usually no maid service. See websites like **airbnb**, **Visit Orlando**, and **HomeAway**.

Many families also report success with house swaps. If you live in Europe, for example, a family in Orlando might be happy to swap their home with yours, saving each of you a considerable amount of money. Swaps are arranged through specialized agencies such as Love Home Swap and Home Link. For a small monthly fee, prospective swappers sign up and list their homes. It is always a good idea to exchange emails, talk on the phone, and trade recent home photos before signing any agreements.

The best times to visit Orlando are October, November, and late February, when the theme parks are least crowded and temperatures are mild. Prices soar during school holidays and are at their peak from late June to August, when temperatures also become sweltering. If you plan to stay in a theme park hotel during these months, it is wise to book at least six months ahead of time.

Before you book your accommodations, check what the listed price covers. Many hotels and resorts add an, often hidden, resort fee of up to $25 a day. The state's 6 per cent sales tax and the tourism tax can greatly increase your costs. Orange County and Osceola County add a 6 per cent tourism tax; and Seminole County (which includes Sanford) adds 5 per cent.

DIRECTORY

SHOPPING

Disney Springs™
☎ 407-939-2273
ⓦ disneysprings.com

Mall at Millenia
☎ 407-363-3555
ⓦ mallatmillenia.com

Orlando International Premium Outlets
☎ 407-352-9600
ⓦ premiumoutlets.com/international

Universal Orlando Resort™
☎ 407-363-8000
ⓦ universalorlando.com

Orlando Vineland Premium Outlets
☎ 407-238-7787
ⓦ premiumoutlets.com/vineland

Walt Disney World®
☎ 407-939-2273
ⓦ disneyworld.com

DINING

OpenTable
ⓦ opentable.com

Universal Orlando Resort™
☎ 407-224-4233

Walt Disney World®
☎ 407-939-1947 (US)
☎ 0800 169 0748 (UK)

ACCOMMODATION

airbnb
ⓦ airbnb.com

HomeAway
ⓦ homeaway.com

Universal Orlando Resort™
☎ 888-273-1311

Visit Orlando
ⓦ visitorlando.com

Walt Disney World®
☎ 407-939-1936

Theme Park Tips

Beat the Crowds

Theme park crowds are thinnest from the second week in September to the third week in November, the first two weeks of December, mid-January to mid-March, and late April through the third week of May. Weekends are always busy.

Tickets

Walt Disney World® allows guests to buy tickets online, saving time waiting in line, but they must be picked up in person. **Universal Orlando Resort™** allows visitors to print out tickets, or you can collect them from the will-call gate for an extra $2.50 per ticket. The online service for **SeaWorld®** lets buyers print out their tickets and, when they arrive at the park, go straight to the turnstiles, where they are verified.

Multiday and Multipark Passes

Disney's Park Hopper and Park Hopper Plus tickets are valid for four to seven days. Both include unlimited entry to the four parks; the Park Hopper Plus tickets also include entry to other Disney attractions. The discounts aren't great, but you save time waiting in line. Universal Studios Florida™, Universal's Islands of Adventure™, Wet 'n Wild®, SeaWorld® Orlando, Aquatica® Water Park, and Busch Gardens® Tampa Bay offer the unlimited-access, 14-day FlexTicket.

Arrival Times

Most theme park attractions open to the public at 9am. Although it may seem sensible to hit the parks as soon as they open and avoid the lines, this is rarely a good idea if you are traveling with small children. Kids who arrive early tend to be exhausted by 2pm and are hard to deal with for the rest of the day. Instead, take it easy in the morning and head for the parks in late afternoon and evenings. Temperatures are cooler, and the parks take on a magical glow under the lights.

Cutting Time in Line

Disney (FastPass+) and Universal and SeaWorld (Express™ Pass) offer a system that cuts out the long wait for the most popular rides and shows. Just slide your ticket through the turnstile to get an allocated spot for your visit. When it's time, simply go to the particular attraction's designated entrance to take your place.

Stroller Rental and Baby Care

All the major theme parks offer stroller rental. There are also excellent nursing facilities, often with free formula provided. Diaper-changing tables can be found in women's and some men's restrooms. Orlando is very family-friendly, so it is generally easy to find facilities.

Getting Wet

Take a change of clothes to the theme parks – if not for yourself, certainly for the children. Apart from water rides where you might expect to get wet, kids enjoy running through "splash areas" to cool off, and it might not always be possible to dry off naturally.

A rain poncho is smart year-round and is worth buying before you get to the parks.

Breaks

Theme parks are tiring at any time of the year but excessively so in summer, when even standing in line can be exhausting. Plan regular breaks at air-conditioned venues or "splash areas", particularly around midday, when the outside temperatures are at their hottest.

Pack a Snack and Water

Theme park prices for refreshments are 30–50 percent higher than you will find outside the parks. The parks prohibit coolers (containers for keeping food and drink cool), but guests can bring bottled water and snacks. There are also a few water fountains dotted around the parks.

Theme Park Ride Restrictions

Disney parks tend to have few health and height restrictions, although Disney Hollywood Studios® is a little limiting. Universal's parks can be more restrictive for younger kids, especially Universal's Islands of Adventure™ (where there are warnings on most of the major rides), but like Universal Studios Florida™, it does have a dedicated kids' area. SeaWorld® has height restrictions on a couple of its rides.

Parent-Swaps

Height restrictions mean that some younger children may not be able to go on certain rides. The theme parks usually have a program that lets one parent ride while the other tends to the kids in a special waiting area; then the second parent can go on the ride. It might not be so much fun riding by yourself, but at least you don't have to wait in line again.

Theme Park Name Tags and Reunion Places

It's very easy to get lost in crowded theme parks. If that happens, find a park employee (they're usually in uniform), and ask for help. Kids aged seven and under should wear tags bearing their name, hotel, and a contact number. Older children and adults should pick a place inside the park to meet if they become separated.

VIP Tours

VIP tours at both **Walt Disney World Resort®** and **Universal Orlando Resort™** take guests on a relatively customized whirlwind tour of the parks. Included is front-row seating for shows, front-of-the-line access to rides and attrac-tions, and your very own tour guide. At Universal, breakfast and lunch, bottled water, and parking are all included; however, the itinerary is slightly less flexible, with a set start and length.

Disney adds door-to-door transportation (picking you up and dropping you back off at your hotel) and a flexible start time, with the ability to add extra time, but no meals are included. Enjoying personalized attention and behind-the-scenes access comes at a price, though, with Disney VIP tours running $400–600 per hour for up to ten guests, with a six-hour minimum, depending on the season, while Universal prices start at $189 per person for group tours, with private-tour costs starting at approximately $1,200.

Behind-the-Scenes Tours

Behind-the-scenes tours are a cheaper way of seeing some of the backstage action.

Walt Disney World® offers a whole host of behind-the-scenes tours, with just a sampling of available tours mentioned here. Disney's Backstage Magic is a comprehensive seven-hour tour that showcases the inner workings of all four theme parks (including the technology behind the attractions at Epcot®, the underground operations of Magic Kingdom®, and more).

Keys to the Kingdom is a five-hour taster tour for guests who would like to see what's on offer before they really get started; it provides a basic park orientation, as well as a glimpse of some of the usually hidden high-tech magic. The Family Magic Tour is a great choice if you have kids along, offering a two-hour scavenger hunt through Disney's most child-friendly park, the Magic Kingdom®.

Places to Stay

PRICE CATEGORIES

For a standard double room per night (with breakfast if included), including taxes and extra charges.

$ under $180 $$ $180–250 $$$ over $250

Theme Park Hotels

Disney's All Star Sports, Music, or Movie Resorts

MAP G1 ▪ 1901 W. Buena Vista Dr ▪ 407-939-7000 ▪ www.disneyworld.com ▪ $$

These family-friendly resorts showcase their themes through Disney characters. The walls and walkways of Movie Resort are adorned with characters from favorite kids' films, while the Music Resort honors country, jazz, rock 'n' roll, calypso, and show tunes. Baseball, football and tennis, among other sports, appear in giant icons in the courtyard at the Sports Resort. Buses are available for guests to visit other theme parks and surrounding areas.

Hilton in the Walt Disney World® Resort

MAP G2 ▪ 1751 Hotel Plaza Blvd ▪ 407-827-4000 ▪ www.hilton.com ▪ $$

The location across from Disney Springs™ just can't be beat. Spacious accommodations coupled with an inviting pool and numerous on-site restaurants make this a popular choice.

Universal's Cabana Bay Resort

MAP E3 ▪ 6550 Adventure Way ▪ 407-503-4000 ▪ www.universalorlando.com ▪ $$

One of Universal's newest resorts boasts a vintage appeal, with mid-century modern styling. Four separate buildings share a lobby and large dining area with counter service. Two large pools and a lazy river, a retro bowling alley, and Jack LaLanne fitness center complete the package. Buses offer free transportation to and from the Universal parks. Early admission to the parks is included.

Disney's Animal Kingdom Lodge & Villas

MAP G1 ▪ 2901 Osceola Pkwy ▪ 407-938-3000 ▪ www.disneyworld.com ▪ $$$

This resort boasts a spectacular lobby with a cathedral-like thatched ceiling. It is adorned with hand-carved furnishings, a three-story clay fireplace, and chandeliers made of African shields. Floor-to-ceiling windows look over the sprawling savanna, where animals roam free. Adding to the appeal are two signature restaurants and unique African- and animal-inspired activities.

Disney's Caribbean Beach Resort

MAP G2 ▪ 900 Cayman Way ▪ 407-934-3400 ▪ www.disneyworld.com ▪ $$$

This Disney resort boasts sprawling grounds, a Spanish fortress-themed pool, bike rentals, a pirate-adventure cruise for kids, campfires, and pirate-themed rooms. On-site dining is in a casual food court. Perks include free Disney transportation (the resort is serviced by Disney's buses), as well as early and after-hours entry to the parks on select days.

Disney's Grand Floridian Resort & Spa

MAP F1 ▪ 4401 Grand Floridian Way ▪ 407-824-3000 ▪ www.disneyworld.com ▪ $$$

Disney's top hotel is an opulent, Victorian-style resort with a refined mood and intimate rooms, some with views of the Magic Kingdom®. Luxurious villas and concierge-level rooms and a location along the monorail add to the appeal. Amenities include a full-service spa and a small marina.

Disney's Port Orleans Resort

MAP F2 ▪ 2201 Orleans Dr ▪ 407-934-5000 ▪ www.disneyworld.com ▪ $$$

This property is two resorts in one. "Riverside" oozes Southern charm, the rooms set in rustic bayou dwellings and Southern-style mansions. The swimming hole on Ol' Man Island boasts rope swings and a Huck Finn appeal. "The French Quarter" has wrought-iron balconies on the buildings, jazz music playing, beautiful gardens, and a Mardi Gras feel. A riverboat provides transportation to the Disney Springs™.

Disney's Swan & Dolphin Resort

MAP F2 ▪ 1500 Epcot Resorts Blvd ▪ 407-934-4000 ▪ www.swan dolphin.com ▪ $$$

Situated between Disney's BoardWalk Inn & Villas and Disney's Yacht and Beach Club resorts, here guests are treated to nicely decorated rooms. There is a sandy beach alongside an inviting pool and waterfall, a full-service spa, and an incredible collection of restaurants – not to mention the number of eateries at nearby resorts. Epcot® is a short walk or water-taxi ride away, as is Disney's Hollywood Studios®.

Holiday Inn Walt Disney

MAP F2 ▪ 1805 Hotel Plaza Blvd ▪ 407-828-8888 ▪ www.hiorlando. com ▪ $$$

This comfortable hotel is a good choice on the Hotel Plaza strip. The glass elevator scales the 14-story, plant-filled atrium and makes for a very exciting ride. There is a free Disney shuttle, free Wi-Fi, and no resort fee.

Loews Portofino Bay Hotel

MAP E3 ▪ 5601 Universal Blvd ▪ 407-224-7118 ▪ www.universalorlando. com ▪ $$$

Inspired by the seaside village of Portofino, Italy, this is Universal's most luxurious resort. A romantic ambience runs through the resort, and some of the well-appointed rooms overlook the harbor and piazza below. A family pool and quiet pool, as well as a Mandara Spa, are among the recreational offerings. Travel by vintage water taxi

to and from the Universal parks, where guests enjoy complimentary Express Pass™ access.

Universal's Hard Rock Hotel

MAP E3 ▪ 5800 Universal Blvd ▪ 407-503-2000 ▪ www.universalorlando. com ▪ $$$

This Universal resort boasts a rock 'n' roll theme with memorabilia in the public spaces. Don't be surprised if you spot a real rock star (or movie star) here, in part thanks to the high-end club and renowned on-site restaurant. Guests at this Mission-style resort enjoy early access and Express Pass privileges at Universal's parks.

Universal's Royal Pacific Resort

MAP E3 ▪ 6300 Hollywood Way ▪ 407-503-3000 ▪ www.universalorlando. com ▪ $$$

With swaying palm trees, winding walkways, and a beautiful lagoon-style pool, this tropical paradise has a Balinese feel. An Emeril's restaurant and a weekly luau are just a sampling of the dining options. Guests enjoy early entry and complimentary Express Pass privileges at the parks, as well as transportation by vintage water taxi.

Universal's Sapphire Falls Resort

MAP E3 ▪ 6601 Adventure Way ▪ 407-503-5000 ▪ www.universalorlando. com ▪ $$$

This Caribbean-themed resort features blue waterfalls, a tropical landscape, and the sound of steel

drums. The charm extends through the resort, from public spaces to the well-appointed rooms, with waterfront dining and a rum bar. Here you will find the largest of Universal's pools, with a spacious deck for soaking up the sun. Perks include early entry to the Universal parks.

Luxury Hotels

Four Seasons Resort Orlando

MAP F2 ▪ 10100 Dream Tree Blvd ▪ 407-313-7777 ▪ www.fourseasons.com/ orlando ▪ $$$

Here guests will find luxury accommodations decorated in pastel hues, along with a full-service spa, meticulously landscaped grounds, an inviting palm-lined pool area, and signature dining. Service is impeccable, and the location makes this the perfect choice for parkgoers with deep pockets.

Gaylord Palms Resort & Convention Center

MAP G2 ▪ 6000 Osceola Pkwy ▪ 407-586-0000 ▪ www.marriott.com ▪ $$$

Located right outside the gates of Disney, this sprawling convention resort has an incredible interior atrium around which stand three distinctively themed areas with well-appointed rooms, many with interior balconies. At the center of the atrium is a miniature version of the Castillo de San Marco, lush gardens, waterfalls, themed restaurants, and a full-service spa, while outside are two beautifully landscaped pools.

Grand Bohemian

MAP P3 ■ 325 S. Orange Ave ■ 407-313-9000 ■ www.grandbohemian hotel.com ■ $$$

In the city of Orlando, away from the theme parks, this grand hotel boasts soft beds, a classy piano bar, and a gallery that showcases works of art. While the exterior is historic, the interior is classically modern.

Hyatt Regency Grand Cypress

MAP F2 ■ 1 Grand Cypress Blvd ■ 407-239-1234 ■ www.grand cypress.hyatt.com ■ $$$

This vast resort is an amazing place to stay. The 18-story atrium has inner and outer glass elevators with great views, some rooms have whirlpool baths, and the resort boasts golf courses, tennis courts, full-service spa, a pool with grottos and waterfalls, and a large lake with a beach, small boats, and fishing.

Hyatt Regency Orlando

MAP F3 ■ 9801 International Drive ■ 407-284-1234 ■ www.orlando. hyatt.regency.com ■ $$$

Expect luxuriously appointed rooms, a Sinatra-esque piano lounge, and a hip yet sophisticated ambience at this resort. A beautifully landscaped pool (well hidden from view), fine dining, and a fabulous 24-hour 1950s-style diner are just some of the offerings here. Once inside, you would never know you are on one of the busiest thoroughfares in Orlando.

Omni Orlando at Championsgate

MAP H1 ■ 1500 Masters Blvd ■ 407-390-6664 ■ www.omnihotels.com ■ $$$

The 15-minute drive to reach here is worth the effort. Here you will find sprawling landscaped grounds, championship golf, a spectacular pool and lazy river set amid towering palms, and impressive accommodations boasting 9-ft (3-m) ceilings and plush amenities.

Ritz Carlton Grande Lakes

MAP F4 ■ 4012 Central Florida Pkwy ■ 407-206-2400 ■ www.grandelakes. com ■ $$$

Away from the theme parks, this luxurious resort boasts exquisitely manicured grounds, posh accommodations, and an Italian flair. A championship golf course, fine dining options, a full-service spa, and lavish pool are just a few of the indulgences here. Sharing the grounds is the JW Marriott next door. This adds a winding and tropically landscaped lazy river, as well as additional restaurants and recreational facilities.

Rosen Shingle Creek

MAP F4 ■ 9939 Universal Blvd ■ 407-996-9932 ■ www.rosenshingle creek.com ■ $$$

This Mediterranean-style resort is located away from the hustle and bustle of the city, set in landscaped grounds and golf courses, and the headwaters of the Florida Everglades.

The rooms and spaces are named for Florida's lakes, rivers, and historical landmarks. Lavishly appointed rooms, a full-service spa, and fine dining are on offer.

Villas of Grand Cypress

MAP F2 ■ 1 N. Jacaranda ■ 407-239-4700 ■ www. grandcypress.com ■ $$$

Sister to the Hyatt Regency Grand Cypress, this secluded resort boasts two championship golf courses, stunning grounds dotted with bright bougainvillea, and one of Orlando's best restaurants. Villas are spacious, each uniquely decorated, some boasting Roman tubs and secluded patios. Away from the crowds, this resort offers a respite from the theme parks and commands a higher price for the privacy offered.

Waldorf Astoria Orlando

MAP G2 ■ 14200 Bonnet Creek Resort Lane ■ 407-597-5500 ■ www.waldorf astoria.hilton.com/ orlando ■ $$$

The Waldorf features meticulously landscaped grounds, oasis-inspired pool, and elegant accommodations coupled with excellent service and amenities. Fine-dining options (mirroring that of the original establishment in New York City) and a full-service spa round out the offerings. A location near Disney makes this a great spot for those park-goers who prefer to stay in stellar off-property surroundings.

Mid-Range Hotels

All Star Vacation Homes
Main Office: MAP G2; 1132 Celebration Blvd; 321-281-4966; www.allstarvacationhomes.com; $$

There are condos and vacation homes in several communities in the tourist districts. With room for up to 16 people, depending on the property, you'll find home theaters, pools, fully equipped kitchens, washers and dryers – in short, all the amenities of a luxury home near the theme parks.

Caribe Royale Resort
MAP G3 ■ 8101 World Center Drive ■ 407-238-8000 ■ www.cariberoyale.com ■ $$

Spacious well-appointed suites and two-bed villas are the norm at this Mediterranean-inspired resort. A full-service spa, fine dining, and array of recreational activities complement the inviting accommodations.

Doubletree Suites
MAP F2 ■ 2305 Hotel Plaza Blvd ■ 407-934-1000 ■ www.doubletree.hilton.com ■ $$

Famous for handing out delicious chocolate-chip cookies on check-in, this all-suite resort boasts spacious accommodations just a few blocks from Disney Springs™.

Floridays Resort
MAP F3 ■ 12562 International Drive ■ 877-821-3018 ■ www.floridaysresortorlando.com ■ $$

This all-suite resort boasts a Mediterranean flavor and all the amenities of home, including plenty of room for families. Large pools, lush landscaped grounds, and theme parks are the big draws.

Liki Tiki Village
17777 Bali Blvd, Winter Garden ■ 407-856-7190 ■ www.likitiki.com ■ $$

Just 7 miles (11 km) from the south gate of Disney, this luxurious complex offers furnished condos. With a vast water park on-site, the kids may never leave for the parks.

Sheraton Vistana Villages
MAP G2 ■ 12401 International Drive South ■ 407-238-5000 ■ www.starwoodhotels.com ■ $$

This condominium-style resort boasts beautiful and luxurious, well-appointed villas with fully stocked kitchens and all the amenities of home – but better. The outdoor grills are spotless.

Marriott World Center
MAP G2 ■ 8701 World Center Drive ■ 407-239-5200 ■ www.marriottworldcenter.com ■ $$$

Located less than 2 miles (3 km) from Disney, this upscale resort caters to business and leisure travelers alike. Boasting well-appointed rooms and suites, numerous on-site dining options, and an extensive pool area, as well as a golf course and full-service spa, you may never need to leave.

Thurston House
MAP K3 ■ 851 Lake Ave ■ 407-539-1911 ■ www.thurstonhouse.com ■ $$$

Built in 1885 and set in woodland just minutes north of Orlando, this quiet, charming B&B is popular with adults. The four rooms overlook Lake Eulalia. It has no pool, but the atmosphere is a winner and it's smoke-free.

Budget Hotels

Best Western Lake Buena Vista
MAP G2 ■ 2000 Hotel Plaza Blvd ■ 407-828-2424 ■ www.bestwestern.com ■ $

This reasonably priced hotel is located within a walking distance from Disney Springs™. Balcony views of the fireworks, along with theme park transportation and free Wi-Fi, make this a bargain.

Coco Key
MAP T2 ■ 7400 International Dr ■ 407-351-2626 ■ www.cocokey-orlando.com ■ No-smoking rooms ■ $

If you like water parks, this family-friendly, pool-centric resort is ideal. A canopy over the kids' pool, high-speed slides for the older ones, free Wi-Fi, and a fitness center are among the highlights.

Comfort Suites Universal Studios
MAP U1 ■ 5617 Major Blvd ■ 407-363-1967 ■ www.comfortsuites.com ■ $

This hotel is just a few minutes from I-Drive, and Universal Studios Florida®. Rooms have refrigerators, microwaves, and Wi-Fi, and breakfast is included.

Drury Inn & Suites

MAP T3 ▪ 7301 Sand
Lake Rd ▪ 407-354-1101
▪ www.druryhotels.com
▪ No-smoking rooms ▪ $

Located conveniently near
the theme parks, this
hotel provides clean
rooms at a bargain price.
Facilities include a fitness
center, Wi-Fi, free breakfast and light supper.

Fairfield Inn & Suites Orlando Lake Buena Vista

MAP G3 ▪ 8615 Vineland
Ave ▪ 407-938-9001
▪ www.marriott.com
▪ No-smoking rooms
▪ $

Part of the landscaped
Marriott Village, this spot
near Disney offers luxury
bedding, a mini-fridge,
free Wi-Fi, a fitness
center, and a pool.

La Quinta Inn & Suites UCF

11805 Research Pkwy
▪ 407-737-6075 ▪ www.
lq.com ▪ $

This hotel, near the
University of Central
Florida, is for guests
who want an east
Orlando location. Rooms
are comfortable, and
rates include breakfast,
local phone calls,
Internet access, and
weekday newspapers.

Rosen Inn

MAP T3 ▪ 6327
International Dr ▪ 800-
999-6327 ▪ www.rosen-
inn6327.com ▪ $

The 315 rooms here
all have refrigerators
and microwaves. There
is also a pool and several
restaurants. Guests
can take the free shuttle
to Universal® Orlando or
SeaWorld® Orlando,
or take the I-Drive trolley.

Rosen Centre®

MAP T3 ▪ 9840
International Drive
▪ 407-996-9840 ▪ www.
rosencentre.com ▪ $$

Indulge yourself in luxury
and tranquility as you
enter the vibrant rooms
of Rosen Centre®. Enjoy
views of the city and
feel right at home with
facilities such as a mini-
refrigerator, coffee maker,
iron and iron board, and
hair dryer. Pet-friendly
and ADA compliant
rooms are available.

Condo and Timeshare Rentals

Blue Tree Resort

MAP F3 ▪ 12007 Cypress
Run Rd ▪ 407-238-6000
▪ www.bluetreeorlando.
com ▪ $

Blue Tree's elegant
and spacious one- and
two-bedroom villas
are well located for
Disney attractions.
The resort has four
pools, two tennis courts,
a volleyball court, and a
playground. Rates are
available with or without
housekeeping services.

Beachtree Villas

MAP G3 ▪ 2545 Chatham
Circle ▪ 407-396-7416
▪ www.beachtreevillas.
com ▪ Smoke-free ▪ $$

Great for families, the
Beachtree Villas has
two- to three-bedroom
homes, each with fully
equipped kitchen and
laundry facilities. There's
an on-site recreation
center, sauna, and a
tennis court, but the
rates do not include
an extra cleaning fee.
Villas have a four-night
minimum stay, while
the houses have a
five-night minimum.

Holiday Villas

7862 W. Irlo Bronson Hwy
▪ 800-344-3959 ▪ www.
holidayvillas.com ▪ $$

For generous living space,
Holiday Villas offers two-
and three-bedroom
condos that can sleep up
to eight, on eight different
properties near Disney.
Each comes with a
washer and dryer.

Marriott Vacation Club International

800-845-5279 ▪ www.
vacationclub.com ▪ $$

Marriott's timeshare
program covers five
Orlando locations. The
apartments and villas can
also be rented by the week.
Some of the villas have
patios or porches, and the
facilities on offer include
activity programs, fitness
centers, golf-course
privileges, tennis courts,
clubhouses, and saunas.

Orlando Breeze Resort

121 Emerald Loop ▪ 1-800-
613-0310 ▪ www.silver
leafresorts.com ▪ Smoke-
free ▪ $$

This resort with two- and
three-bedroom villas is a
home away from home.
It has none of the crowds
or tourist frenzy of the
mainstream areas.

Parkway Palms Resorts

3100 Parkway Blvd
▪ 407-396-8484 ▪ www.
palmscondovillas.com
▪ $$

This company rents out
accommodation through
AirBnB and booking.com
and also offers something
for everyone, from hotel
rooms, private homes,
apartments, town homes
to private rooms near
famous attractions.

Sheraton's Vistana Resort

MAP G2 ■ 8800 Vistana Center Dr ■ 407-239-3100 ■ www.starwood.com/sheraton ■ $$

This resort offers modern one- and two-bedroom villas and townhouses, packed with home comforts, for rent by the week. The tennis facilities are excellent, with clay and all-weather courts.

Summer Bay Resort

MAP G1 ■ 17805 W. Irlo Bronson Memorial Hwy ■ 855-849-2205 ■ www.summerbayresort.com ■ $$

Accommodations at Summer Bay range from one-bed condos to three-bed villas, all with washers and dryers. The property has a clubhouse and offers water sports.

Disney Vacation Club®

MAP F2, G2 & F1 ■ 800-800-9100 ■ www.dvcresorts.com ■ $$$

The same upscale Disney units sold as timeshares are also available to rent. Properties are on land owned by Disney, such as Old Key West Resort, Animal Kingdom Lodge, and BoardWalk Villas.

Close to Nature

The Camp sites at Disney's Fort Wilderness Resort

MAP F1 ■ 4501 N. Fort Wilderness Tr ■ 407-824-2900 ■ www.disneyworld.com ■ $

Located across the Magic Kingdom®, this 750-acre (3-sq-km) country retreat offers a range of camp sites with amenities similar to Disney's high-end resorts. Winding trails through the woods reveal spectacular pools and Disney characters perform around a campfire.

Clerbrook Golf & RV Resort

20005 Hwy 27 ■ 352-394-5513 ■ www.clerbrook.com ■ $

This large site, popular with golfers, offers 1,250 RV hook-ups, as well as non-smoking villas. Amenities include a driving range, whirlpool spa, shuffleboard, swimming pool, horseshoes, basketball court, and more.

Floridian RV Resort

5150 Boggy Creek Rd ■ 407-892-5171 ■ www.florida-rv-parks.com ■ $

This woodsy retreat near East Lake Tohopekaliga has full hook-ups for RVs, two clubhouses, a playground, tennis courts, and a volleyball court. Leisure activities in the area include airboat rides and parasailing.

Kissimmee/Orlando KOA

2644 Happy Camper Pl ■ 407-396-2400 ■ www.koa.com ■ $

This is a great spot if you want to be close to Walt Disney World® and SeaWorld®. There are RV sites, camp sites, and cabins. The RV sites can have cable TV and modem dataport connected for an extra charge.

Orlando Southwest Fort Summit KOA

2525 Frontage Rd ■ 863-424-1880 ■ www.fortsummit.com ■ $

This resort offers hook-ups for RVs, as well as small timber cabins and pitches for tents. There's a store, laundromats, and Internet access.

Orlando Winter Garden RV Resort

MAP C1 ■ 13905 W. Colonial Dr ■ 407-656-1415 ■ www.wintergardenrv.com ■ $

Pines and ponds are all around this RV resort, about a 30-minute drive from Walt Disney World®. A premier destination for campers for recreational activities, the resort also boasts lots of facilities, such as laundry, games room, dances, bingo, and barbecues. Popular with an older crowd.

Southport Park Campground & Marina

2001 E. Southport Rd ■ 407-933-5822 ■ www.southportpark.com ■ $

This park is in 25-acres (100,000 sq km) of lakeside woods. While away the time by fishing, wandering among the wildlife (such as deer and eagles), or taking an airboat trip. There are RV and tent sites with full hook-ups.

Circle F. Dude Ranch Camp

Hwy 60 & Dude Ranch Rd ■ 863-676-4113 ■ www.circlefduderanchcamp.com ■ smoke-free ■ $$

This kids' summer camp is also a family retreat on selected weekends between November and May. Enjoy the rustic, bunkhouse-style cabins, located around lush oaks and lakeside. Hay rides, horseback riding, lake swimming, and sailing are some of the activities on offer.

General Index

Money 136
Moore, Henry 47
Morocco World Showcase Pavilion 19
Morse (Charles Hosmer) Museum of American Art 47, 125, 127
Motorbikes 61
Mount Dora 90
Multiday passes 140
Multipark passes 140
Muppet™ Vision 3-D 21
Museums and galleries 46–7
Albin Polasek Museum and Sculpture Gardens 47, 127
Charles Hosmer Morse Museum of American Art 47, 125, 127
Cornell Fine Arts Museum 47, 126, 127
Grand Bohemian Gallery, The 47, 85
Henry B. Plant Museum 89
Historic Waterhouse Residence and Carpentry Shop Museum 126
Holocaust Memorial Resource & Education Center 47
Madam Tussaud's 106
Maitland Art Center 47
Mennello Museum of American Art 46, 120, 121
Museum of Military History 116
Orange County Regional History Center 46, 121

Museums and galleries (cont.)
Orlando Museum of Art (OMA) 46, 119, 121
Orlando Science Center 46, 119, 121
Osceola Arts 49, 116
Pioneer Village at Shingle Creek 113
Ripley's Believe It or Not!® Odditorium 52, 103, 106
Salvador Dalí Museum 88
Telephone Museum 47
Titanic: The Artifact Exhibition 53, 105
Music 48
free events 84
live music venues 68–9
Music at Harbor Piazza, Loews Portofino Bay Hotel 84
Mystic Fountain, The 32

N
Name tags, in theme parks 141
NASA 38, 42–3
National Historic Landmarks
Bok Tower Gardens 89
Natural springs 57
Nèu Lotus Spa at the Renaissance Orlando at SeaWorld® 59
New Smyrna Beach 90
Newspapers 136, 137
Nicklaus, Jack 63
Night of Joy 87
Nightlife
Downtown Orlando 122
gay and lesbian nightlife 72–3
International Drive Area 108

Nightlife (cont.)
Walt Disney World® Resort and Lake Buena Vista 99
Winter Park, Maitland and Eatonville 128
Nightime Lights at Hogwarts™ Castle, The 35
Norman, Greg 62, 63
Norway World Showcase Pavilion 19

O
Off the beaten path 64–5
O'Keeffe, Georgia 46
Old Town (Kissimmee) 114
Ollivanders™ 35
One Fish, Two Fish, Red Fish, Blue Fish™ 32
Opening hours 136–7
Orange County Regional History Center 46, 121
Orlando Ballet 49
Orlando City Soccer 61
Orlando International Fringe Festival 49
Orlando Magic 61
Orlando Museum of Art (OMA) 52, 119, 121
Orlando Orchestra Fringe Festival 86
Orlando Philharmonic 48
Orlando Pride 61
Orlando Repertory Theater 48
Orlando Science Center 46, 119, 121
Orlando Shakes 48
Orlando Tree Trek Adventure Park 116
Orlando Watersports Complex 52
Osceola Arts 49, 116
Outdoor activities 60–61

Acknowledgments

The Authors

Richard Grula lives in Orlando and specializes in writing about the Downtown and cultural scenes. He's contributed to the *Orlando Weekly*, *Orlando Magazine*, *Sidewalk.com*, and *Time Out's Guide to Miami and Orlando*.

Jim and Cynthia Tunstall are Central Florida natives who have written five other Florida guides, including Frommer's *Walt Disney World & Orlando*.

Additional contributor
Laura Lea Miller

Publishing Director Georgina Dee

Publisher Vivien Antwi

Design Director Phil Ormerod

Editorial Sophie Adam, Kate Berens, Michelle Crane, Rebecca Flynn, Rachel Fox, Sally Schafer, Akanksha Siwach

Cover Design Maxine Pedliham, Vinita Venugopal

Design Tessa Bindloss, Bharti Karakoti, Bhavika Mathur, Ankita Sharma, Vinita Venugopal

Picture Research Sumita Khatwani, Ellen Root

Cartography Suresh Kumar, Casper Morris, Reetu Pandey, John Plumer

DTP Jason Little

Production Igrain Roberts

Factchecker Jennifer Greenhill-Taylor

Proofreader Kathryn Glendenning

Indexer Hilary Bird

Illustrator Lee Redmond

First edition created by Departure Lounge, London

Revisions Mohammad Hassan, Shikha Kulkarni, Margaret Musial, Gaurav Nagpal, Bandana Paul, Azeem Siddiqui, Manjari Thakur, Priyanka Thakur, Stuti Tiwari

Commissioned Photography Steven Greaves/ Scenic Boat Tour 125b, Magnus Rew/Albin Polasek Museum and Sculpture Gardens, Orlando 127cl, /Four Points Sheraton Hotel, Orlando 117cl, /Boheme, Orlando 77cr, Rough Guides/Dan Bannister

Picture Credits

The publisher would like to thank the following for their kind permission to reproduce their photographs:
Key: a-above; b-below/bottom; c-centre; f-far; l-left; r-right; t-top

Alamy Stock Photo: AA World Travel Library 128t; Stuart Abraham 104b; age fotostock 7tr, 91bl; America 60b; Todd Anderson 53tr; Sandra Baker 11br; Pat Canova 86b; Yvette Cardozo 16bc; Humberto Olarte Cupas 96b; Ian Dagnall 53tr, 55tl, 112c; Michael DeFreitas 54cl; Doug Diamond 69br; Disney Magic 31cr; Philip Duff 61cl; GALA Images 1; Greg Balfour Evans 97cl; Findlay 85tr,120b; Carrie Garcia 84c; Carrie Garcia 118tl; Jeff Greenberg 6 of 6 78t; Helen Sessions 98br; Hemis 56clb; Paul Hennessy 60tl, 97br; Dan Highton 20cra, 99tl; Robert Hoetink 106b; Allan Hughes 38cla,103br; imageBROKER 95tr; Marty Jean-Louis 71tl; Andre Jenny 95bl; JHP Travel 11cr; Keith Levit 108bl; Shine-a-light 114c; Mira 89bl; M. Timothy O'Keefe 79tr, 85clb,101cla, 120tl; David Osborn 52t; Sean Pavone 3tl, 91t, 92-3; Jeremy Pembrey 21br; Prisma Bildagentur AG 19bl; Mervyn Rees 4crb; RosaBetancourt 0 people images 83br, 98cl; RosalreneBetancourt 5 82cl, 115tll; RosalreneBetancourt 6 121cl; RosalreneBetancourt 8 113br; RSBPhoto1 2tr, 3tr, 4clb, 11tl, 15tr, 28tr, 31tr, 32tr, 32bl, 44-5, 50bl, 51tr, 78bc, 83tl,103tl, 130-1; James Schwabel 38-9; Stephen Searle 4cla, 4t, 10c, 11ca, 24 -5, 29c, 65b; Helen Sessions 10cla; Stock Connection Blue 54b, 56t; Torontonian 74tr; Travel Pictures 124cla; D. Trozzo 23br; Universal Images Group North America LLC 2tl; 8-9; WWPICS / Kike Calvo 17crb; Jim West 39cl; Gregory Wrona 88cl, 126bl; Zoonar GmbH 26cla; ZUMA Press Inc 14t, 61tr, 76br, 89tr, 107cr, 123bl, 76br.

Cornell Fine Arts Museum: 126t.

Creative City Project: 87cl.

Cuba Libre Restaurant & Rum Bar: 108cr.

© Disney: 4cr, 12cl, 13bc, 15cl, 16cl, 16-7, 21tl, 22-3c, "The Twilight Zone™ is a registered trademark of, CBS, Inc. and is used pursuant to a license from, CBS, Inc." 51clb, 57c, 63tl.

Dreamstime.com: Tony Bosse 100t; Lucy Clark 20clb, 30-1; Jerry Coli 21cra, 90tl; Crackerclips 52bl; Michael Gordon 4cl; Wangkun Jia 10crb, 29b; Megan Kasper 30bl; Kmiragaya 10bl; Mfschramm 10cl; Nlizer 14bc; Sean Pavone 4b; Mike Ricci 12-3, 21; Szilkov 12br, 50tr; David Watkins 38cr; Jeff Whyte 18c, 19cr; Wisconsinart 6cla, 23tl.

Forever Florida & Allen Broussard Conservancy: 64tl, 114b.

Four Seasons Resort Orlando: 58b, 63cr.

Getty Images: Blaine Harrington III 18t; Panoramic Images 11crb; joe daniel price 84t.

Hard Rock Live Orlando: 69t.

Hard Rock Orlando: 81cr.

Howl at the Moon: 69c.

ICEBAR Orlando: 70b.

Kennedy Space Center: 40cla, 40br, 40-1, 41tl, 43tl, 90cl.

La Cava Tequila: 80tr.

Legoland Florida: 36cl, 36-7, 37crb, 110–1, 113tl; Chip Litherland Photography Inc 36br.